THE TATTOO COLOURING BOOK II

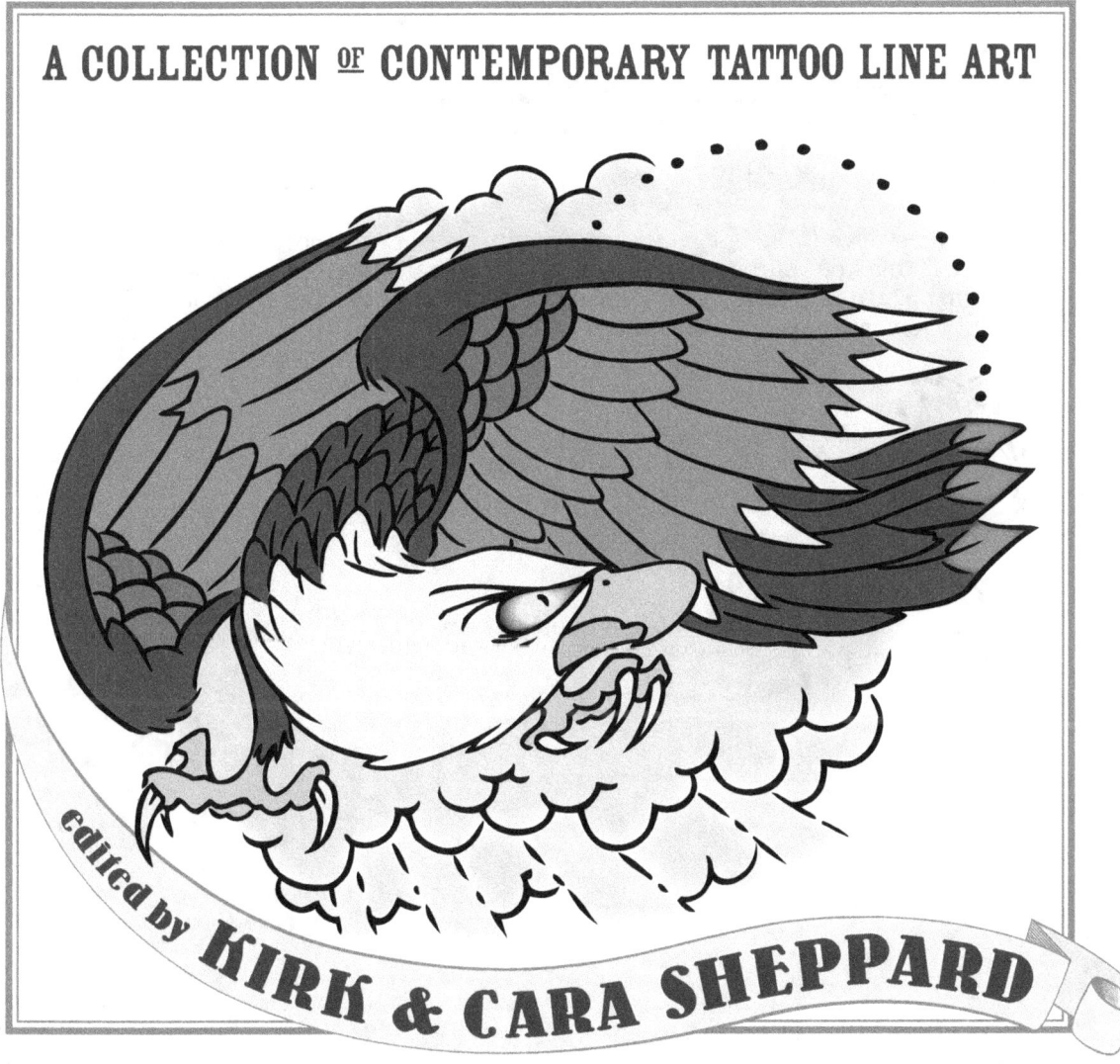

A COLLECTION OF CONTEMPORARY TATTOO LINE ART

edited by KIRK & CARA SHEPPARD

TO THE TATTOOERS OF TODAY,
LOOKING TO THE PAST WHILE
FORGING A PATH TO THE FUTURE.

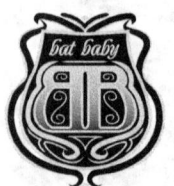

Cover design and page layout
by Cara Sheppard for Bat Baby
www.bat-baby-design.com

Printed and distributed by Lulu, www.lulu.com
Wholesale inquiries to cara@bat-baby-design.com

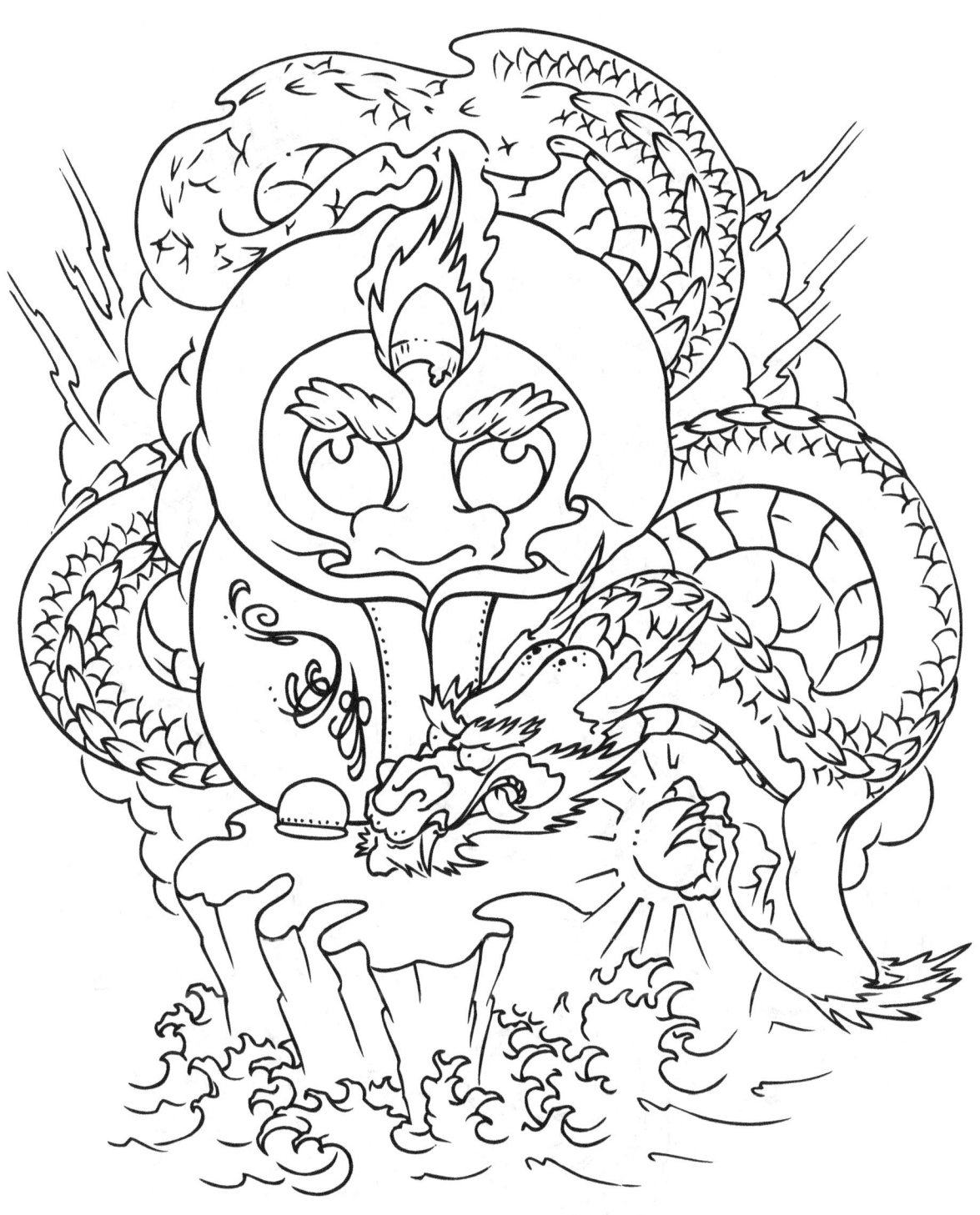

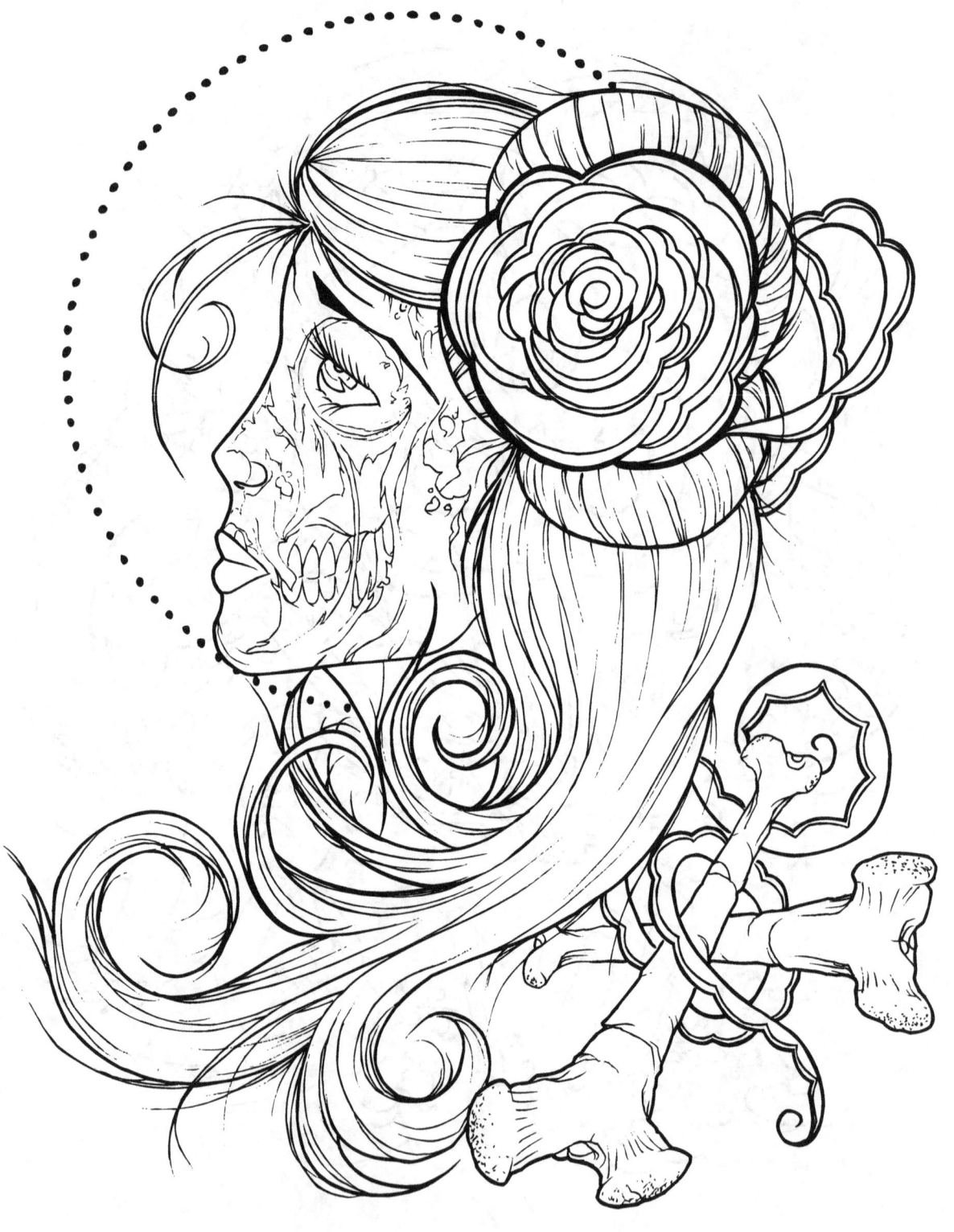

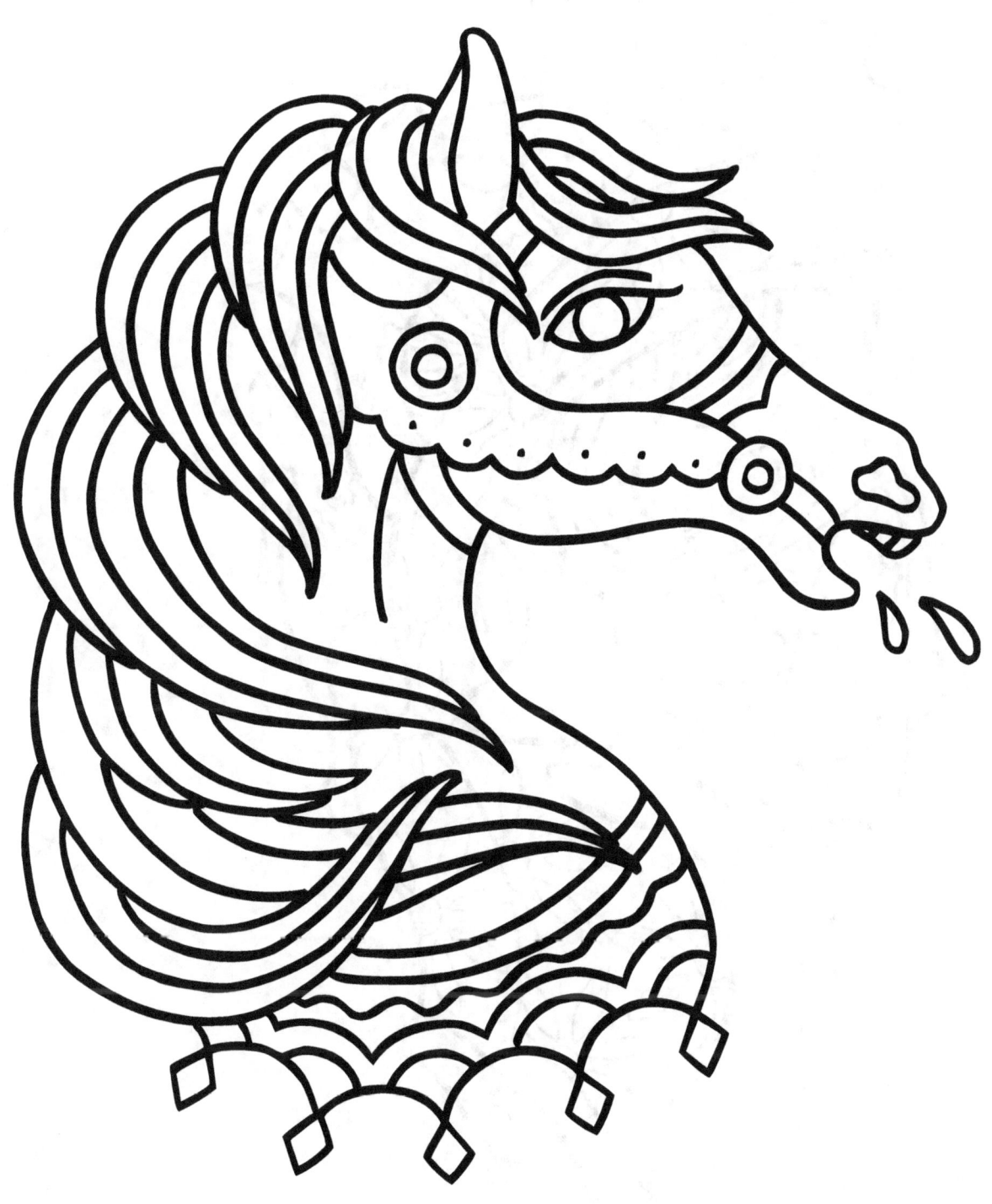

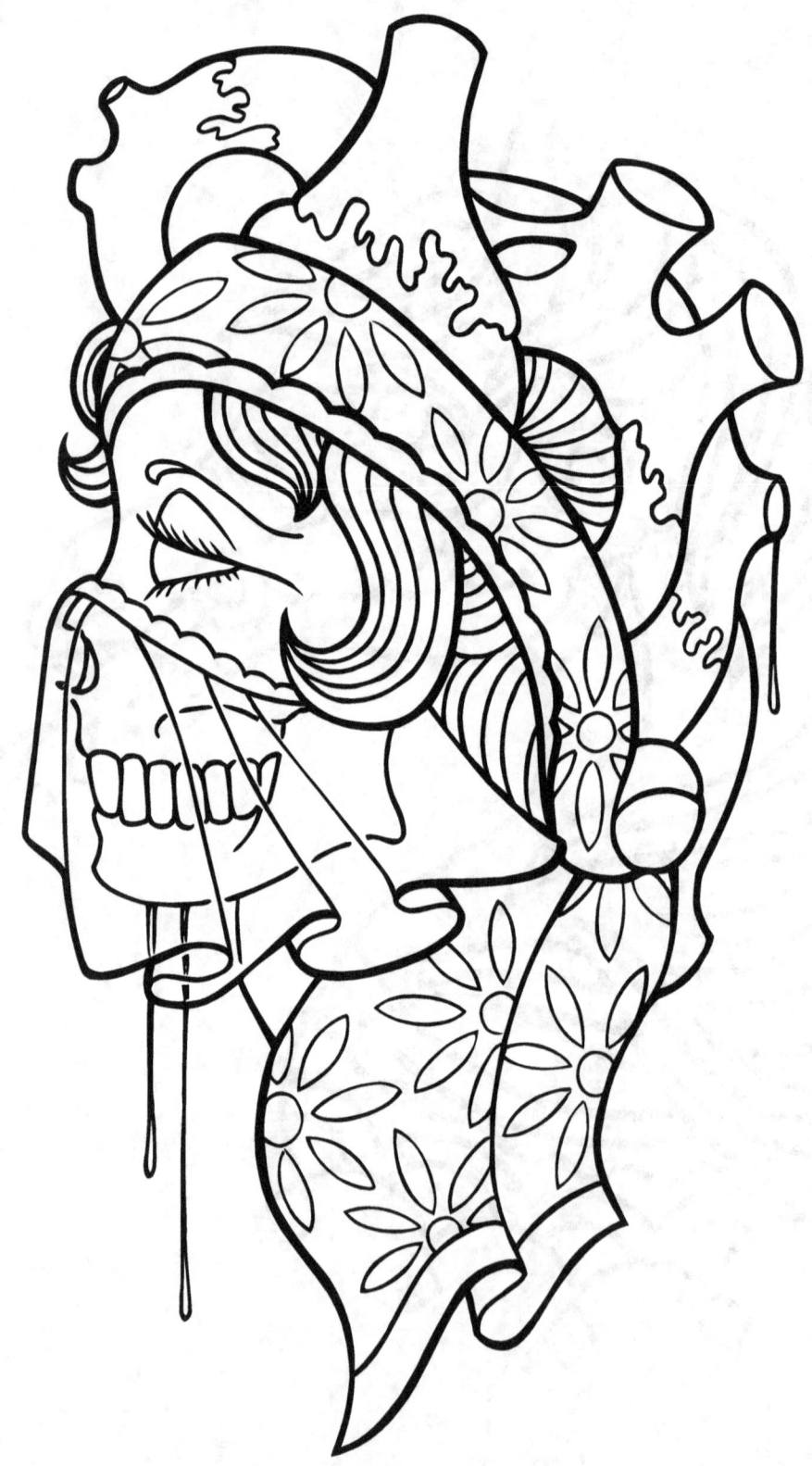

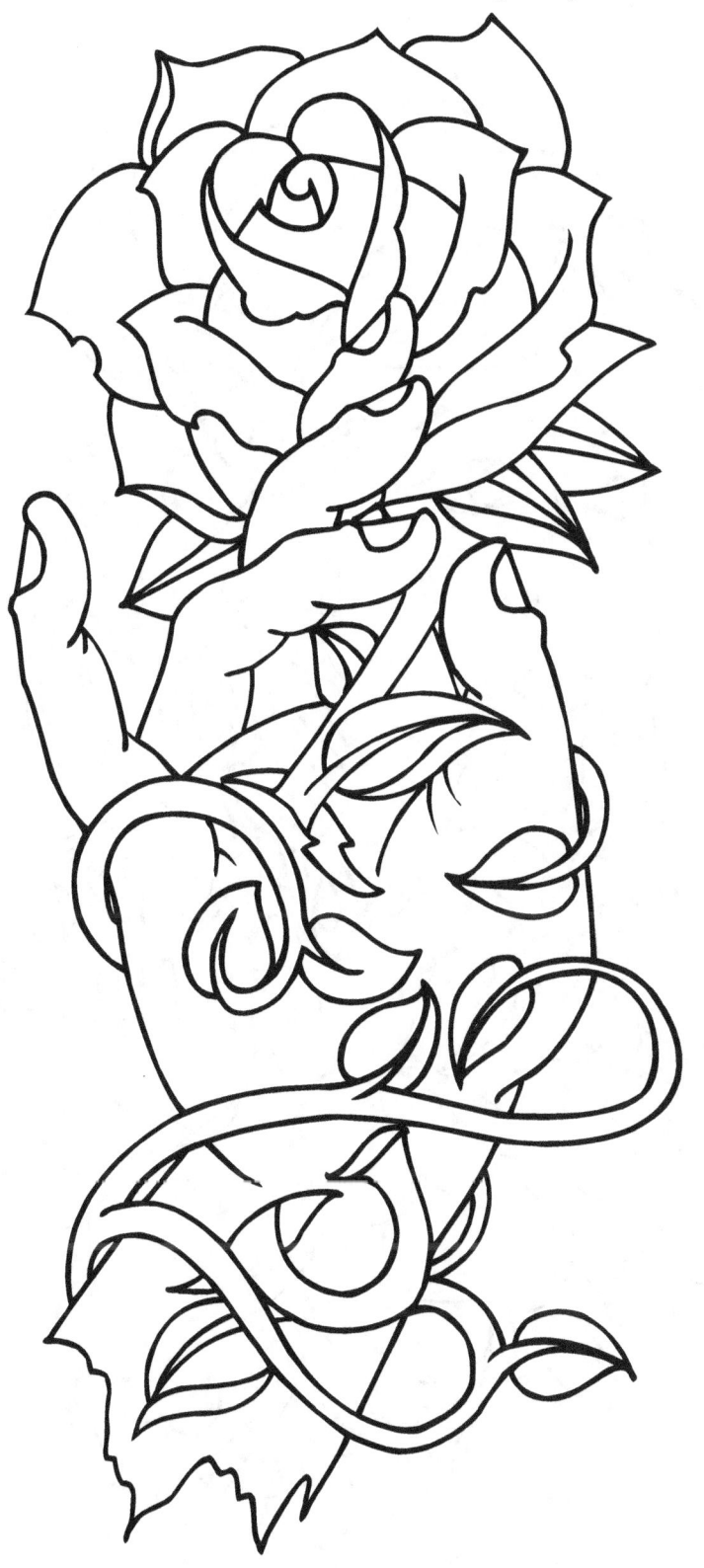

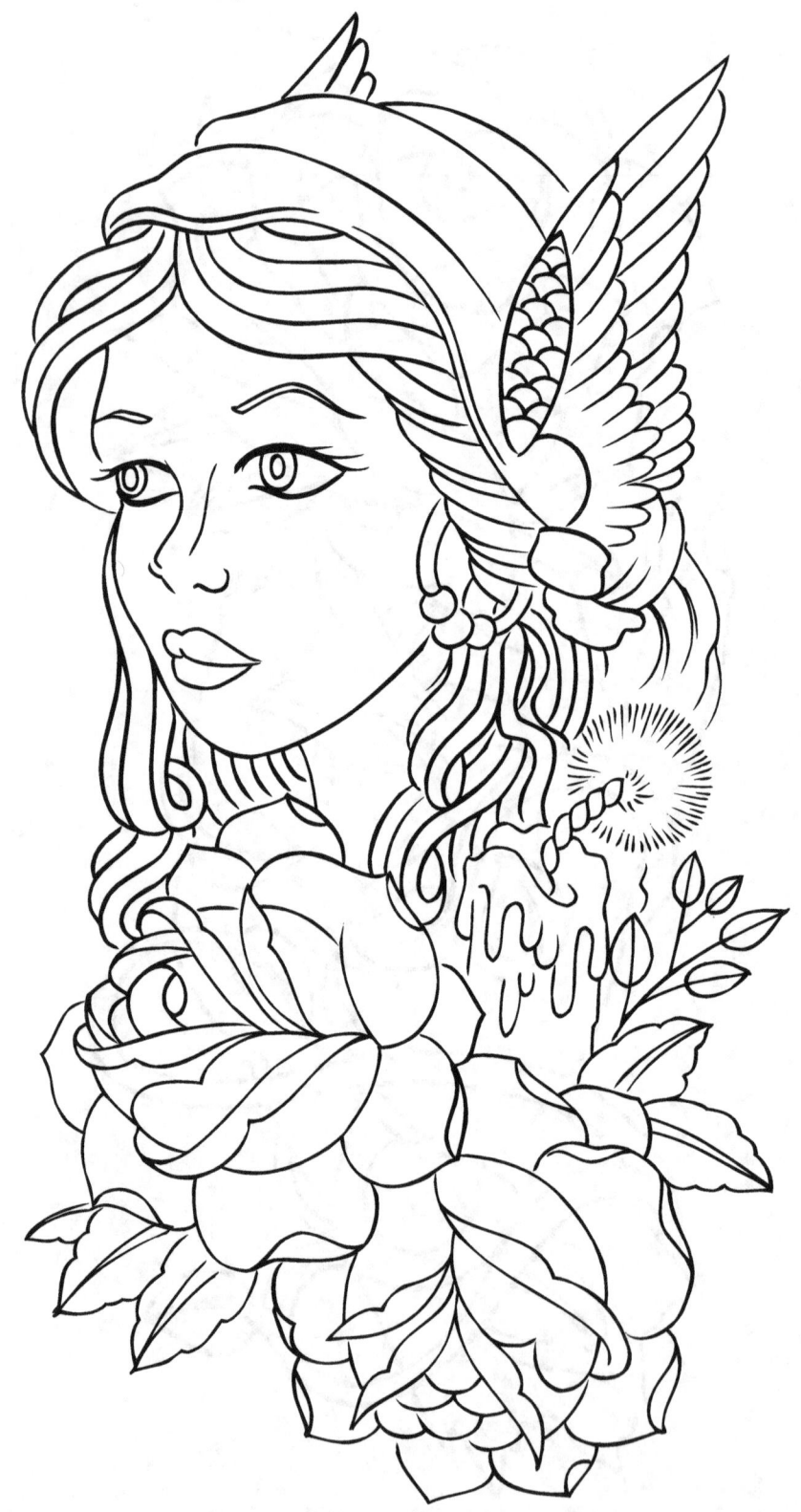

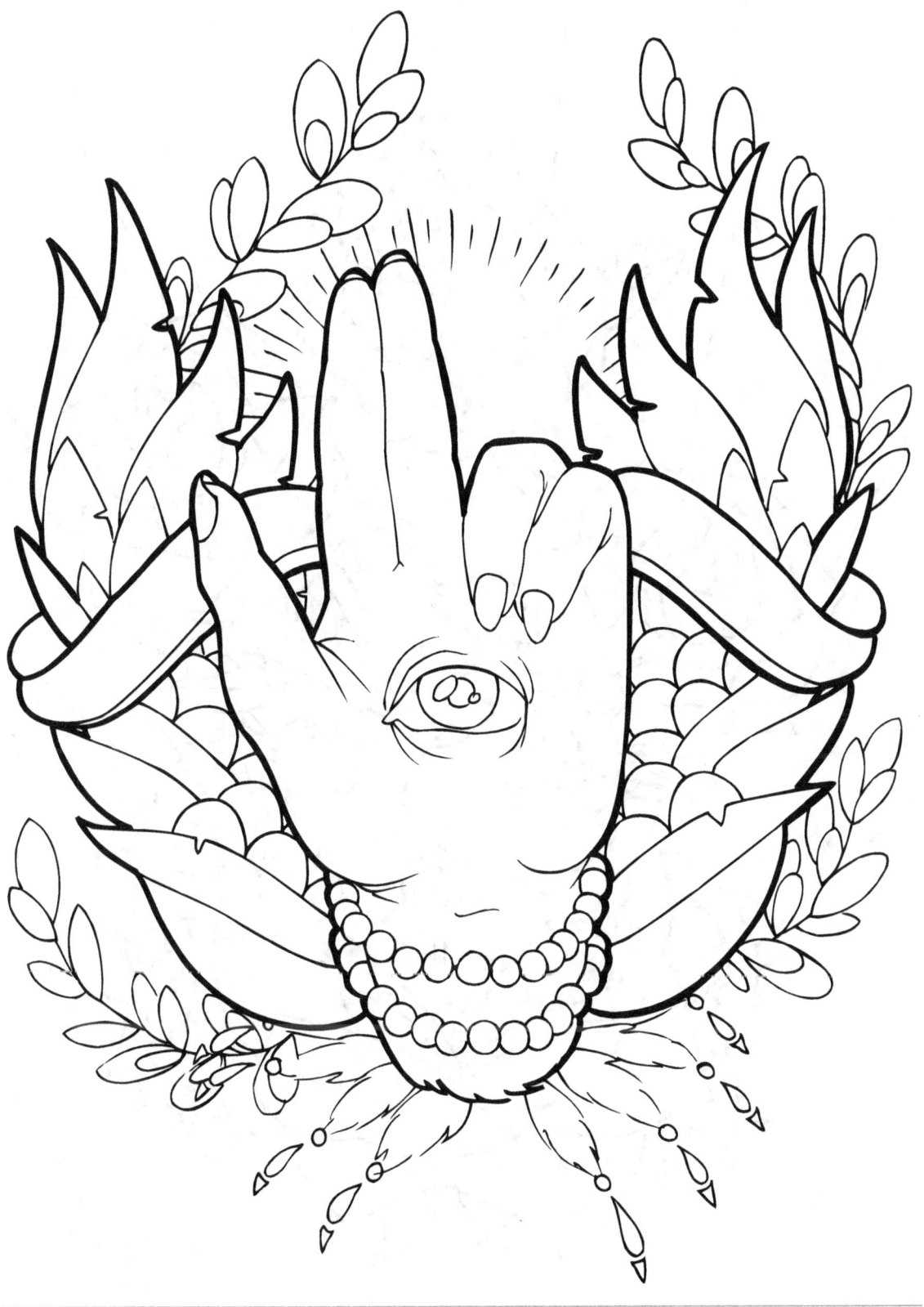

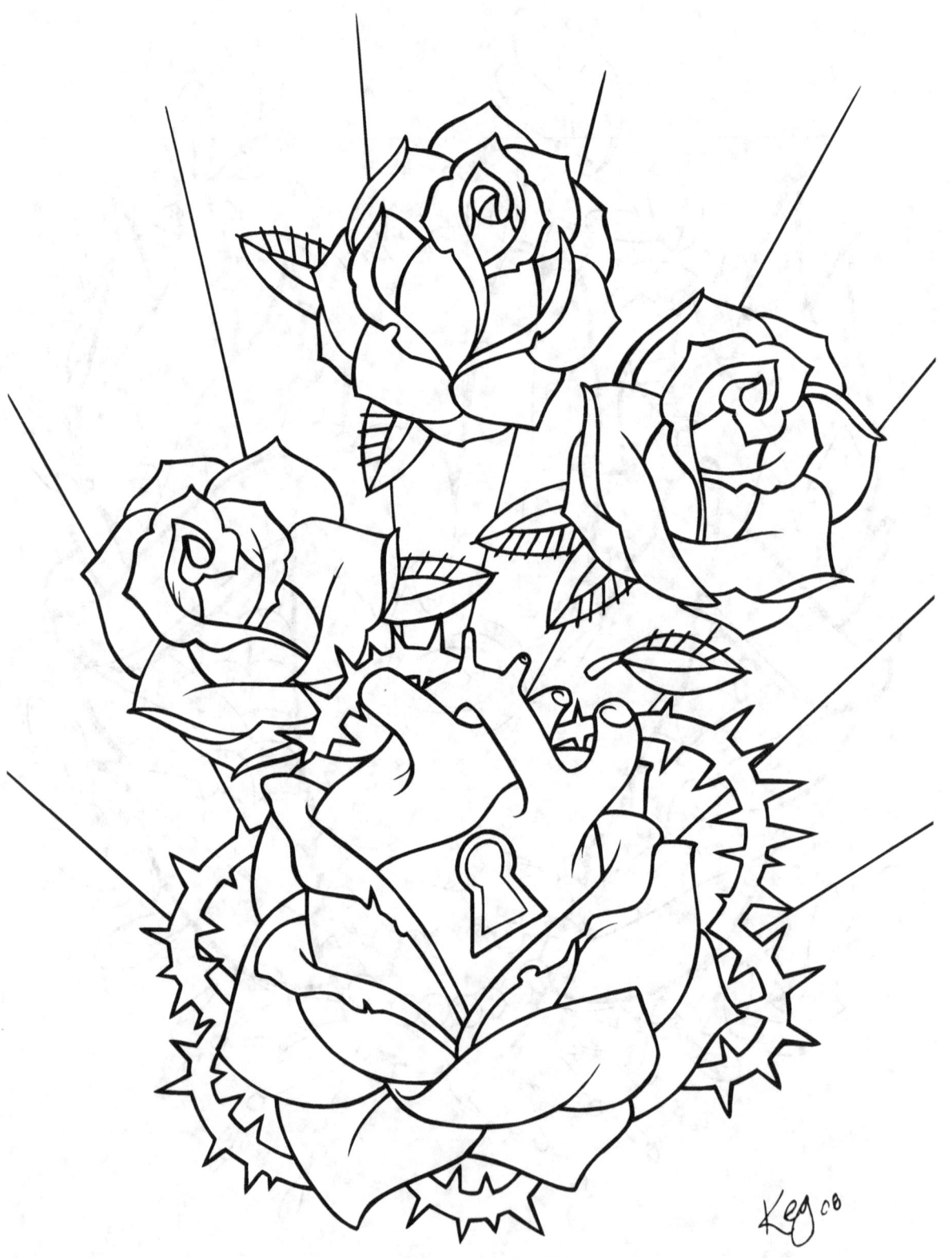

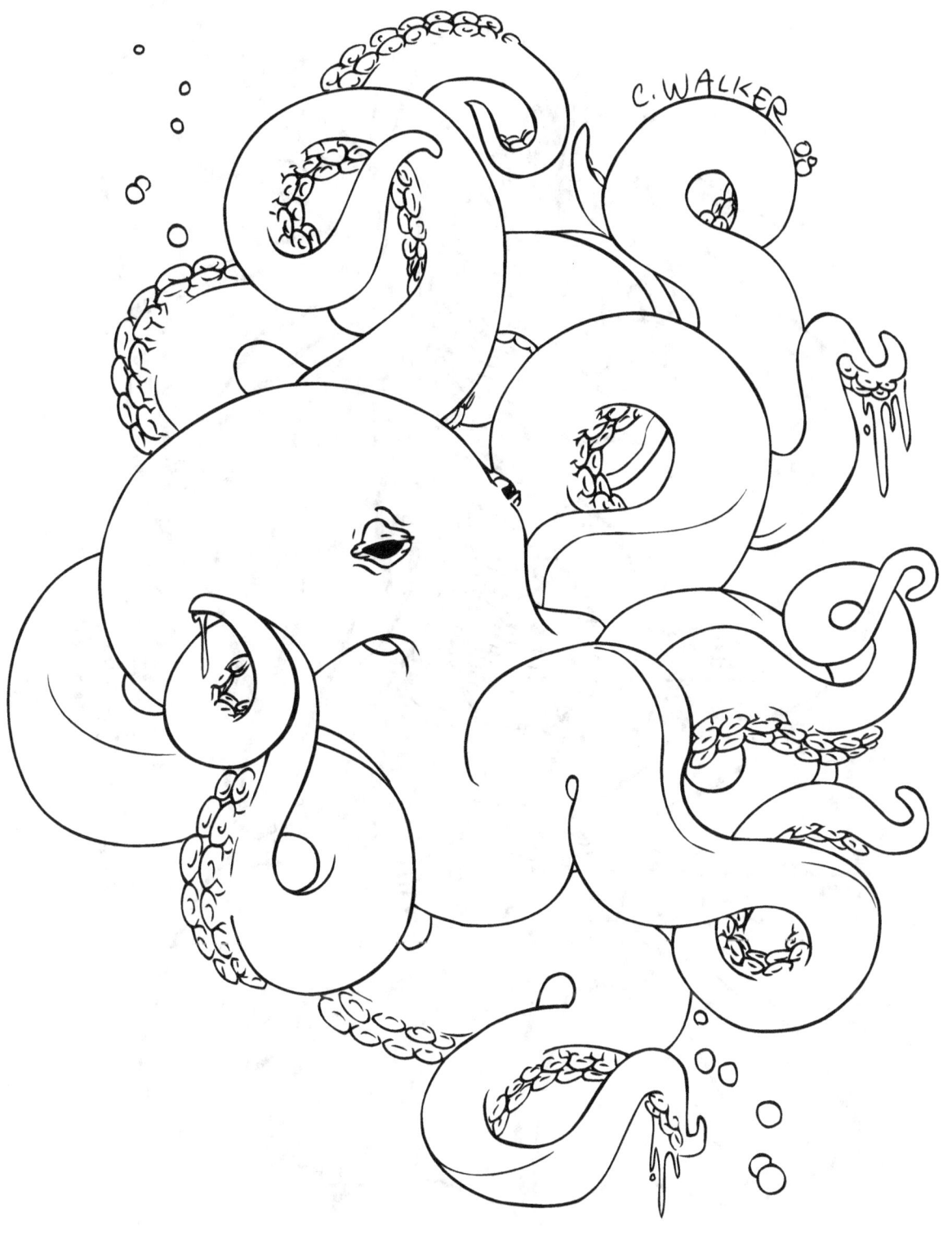

C.WALKER

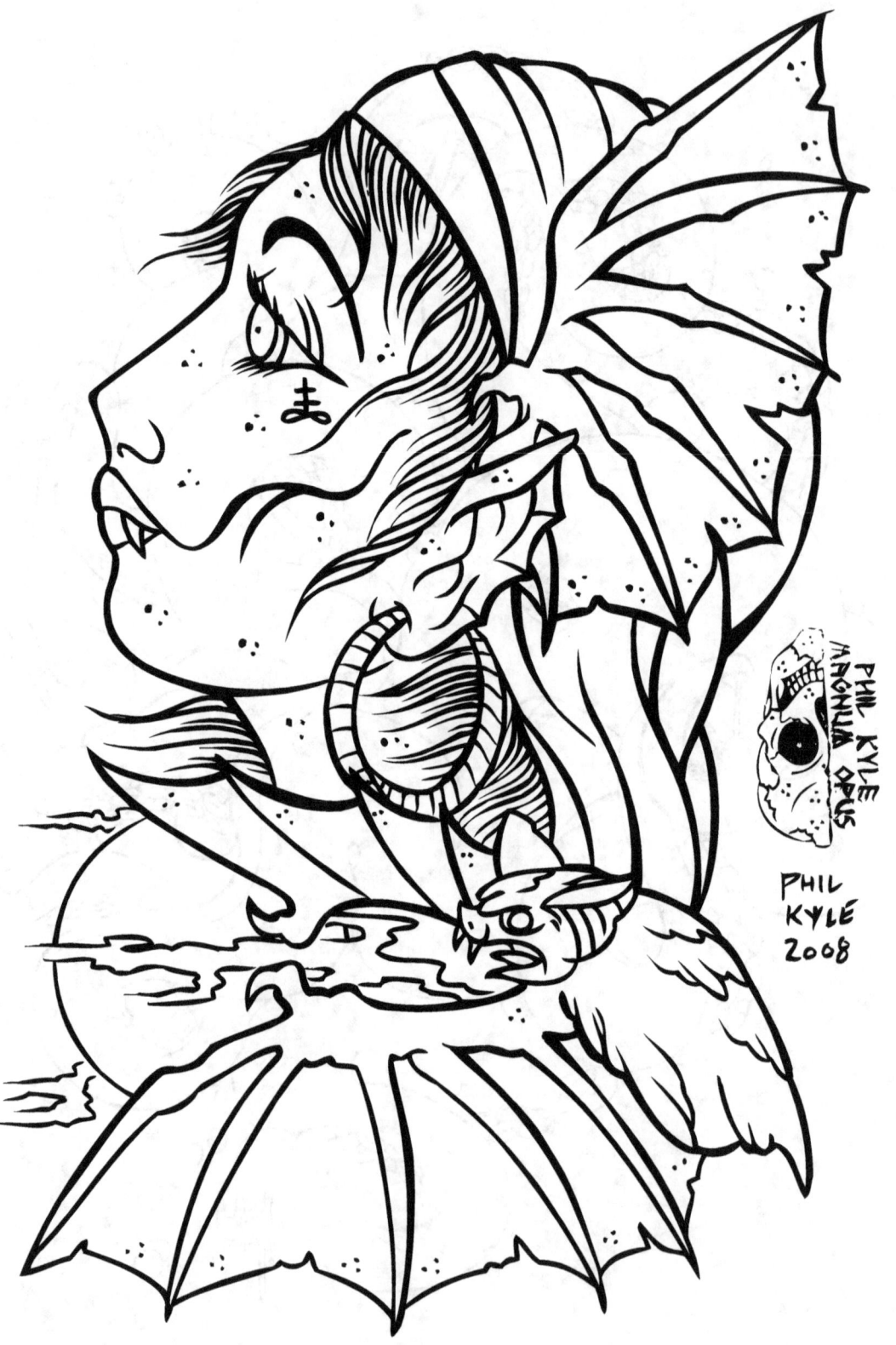

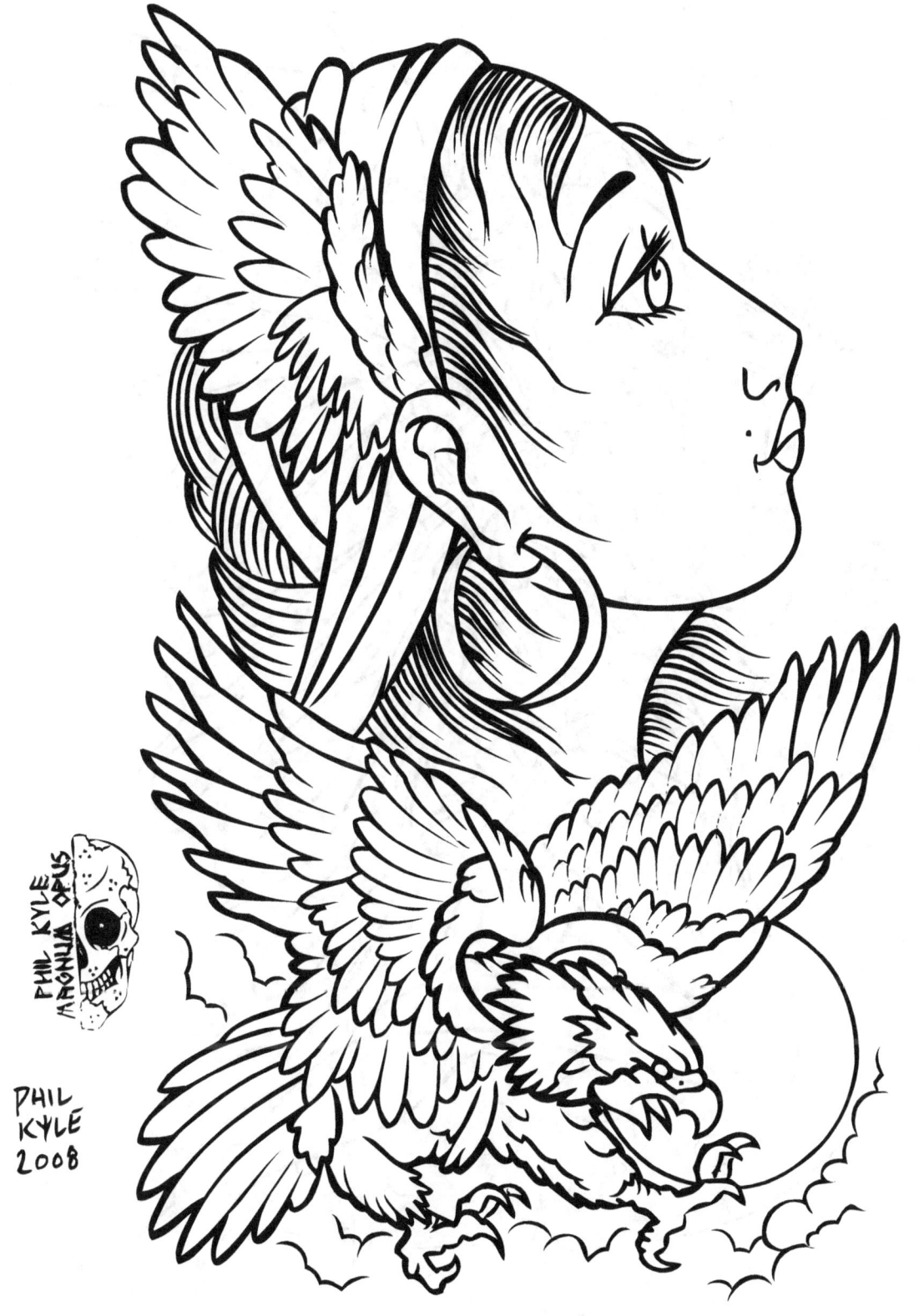

PHIL KYLE
2008

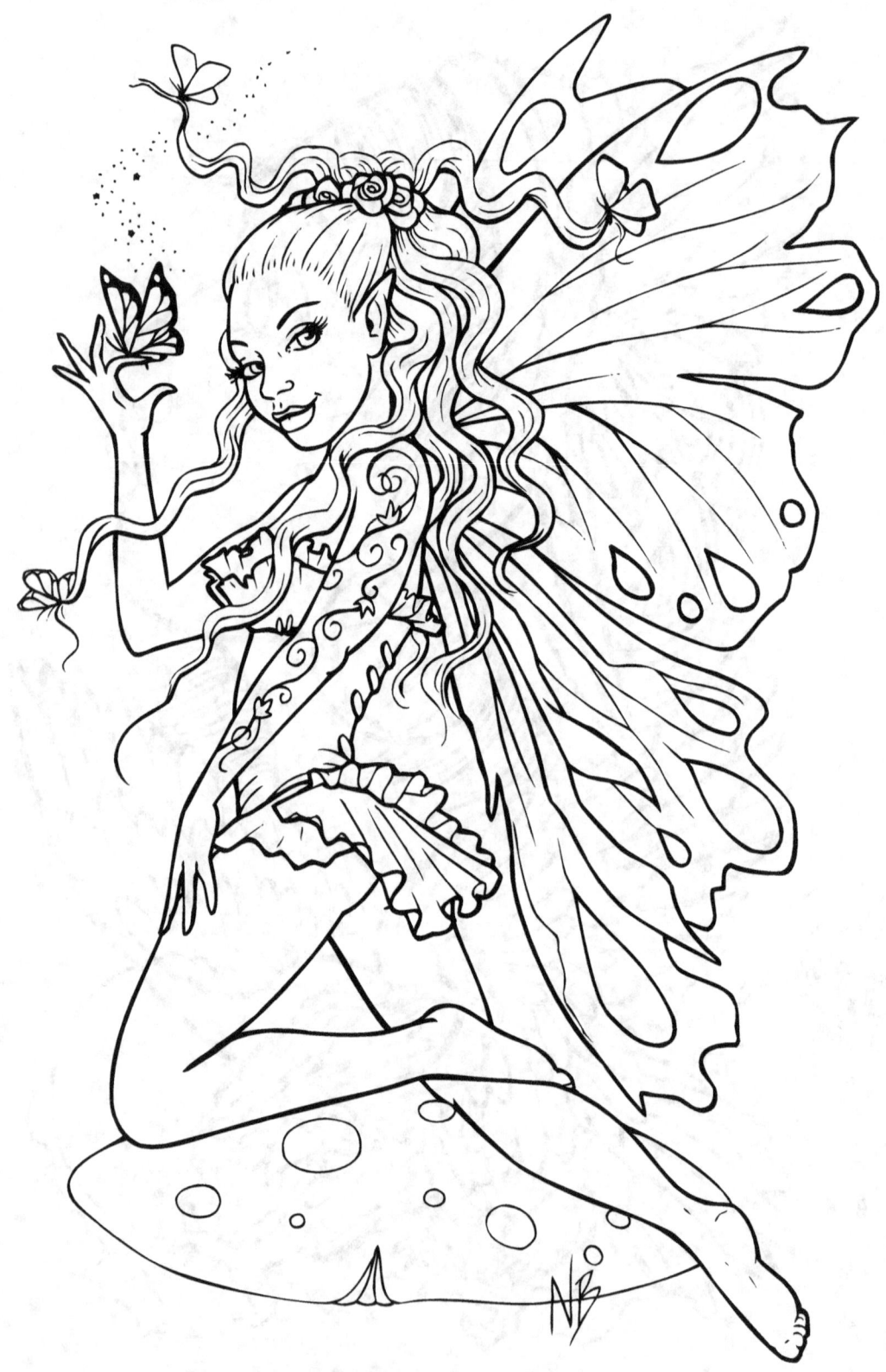

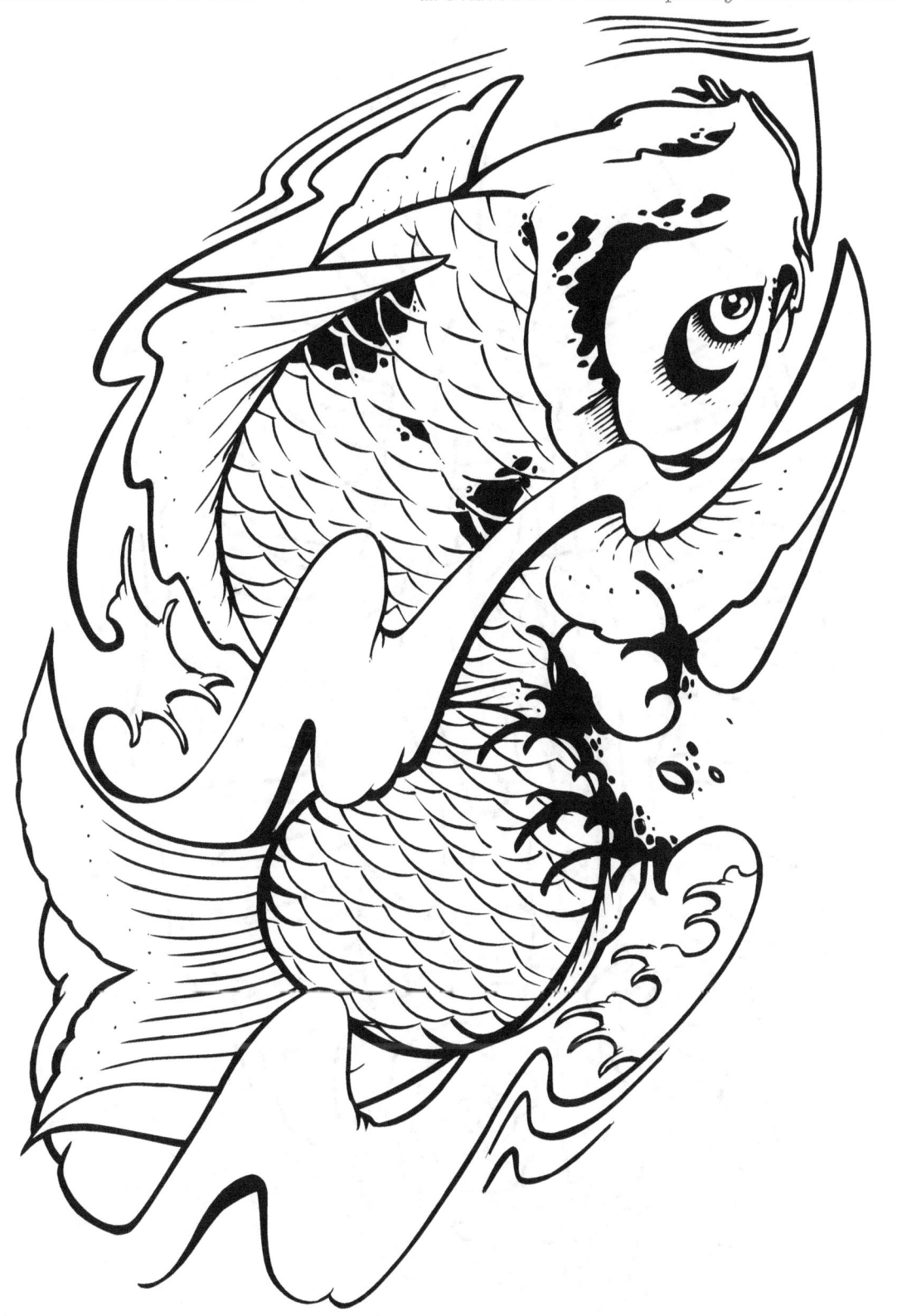

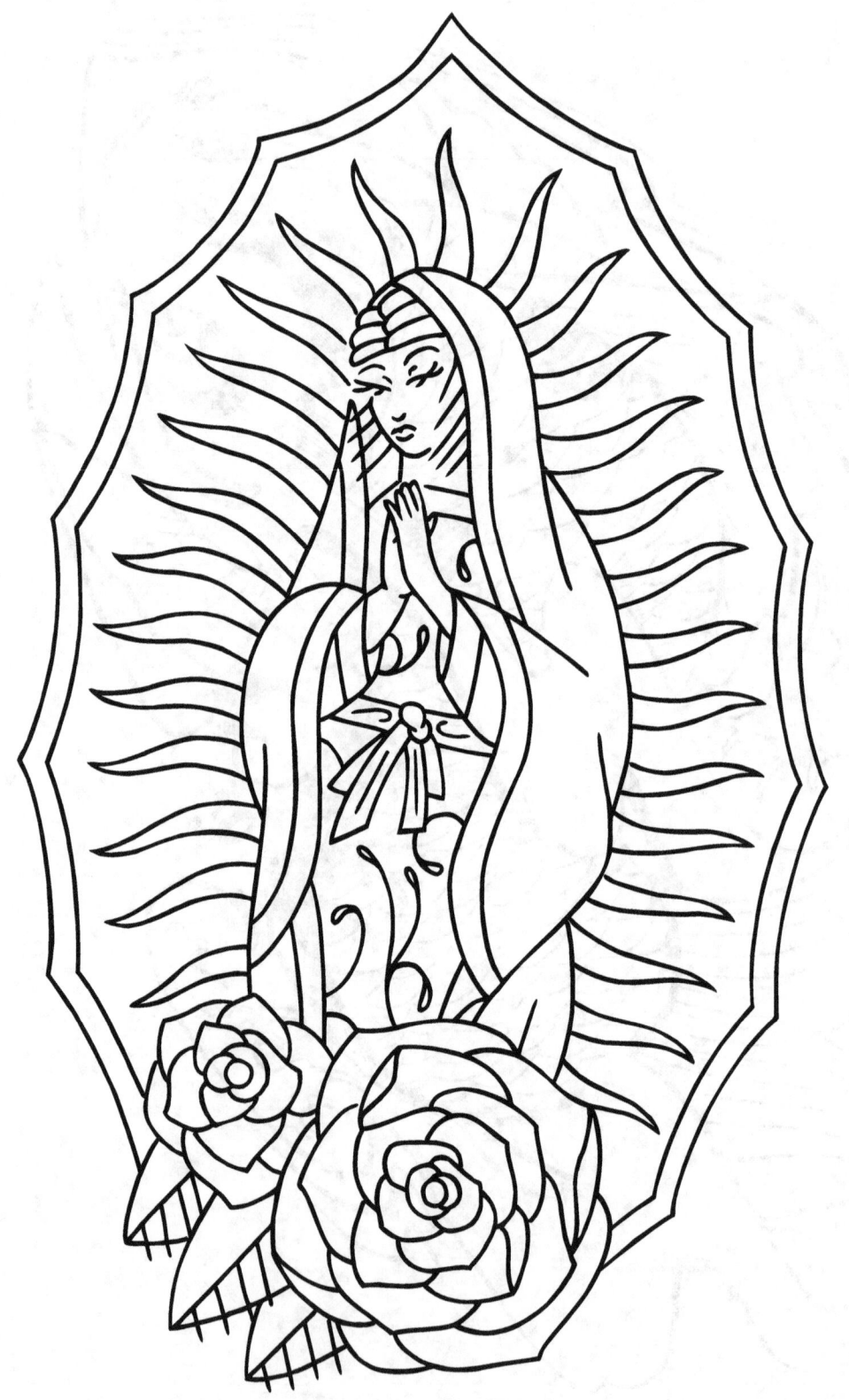

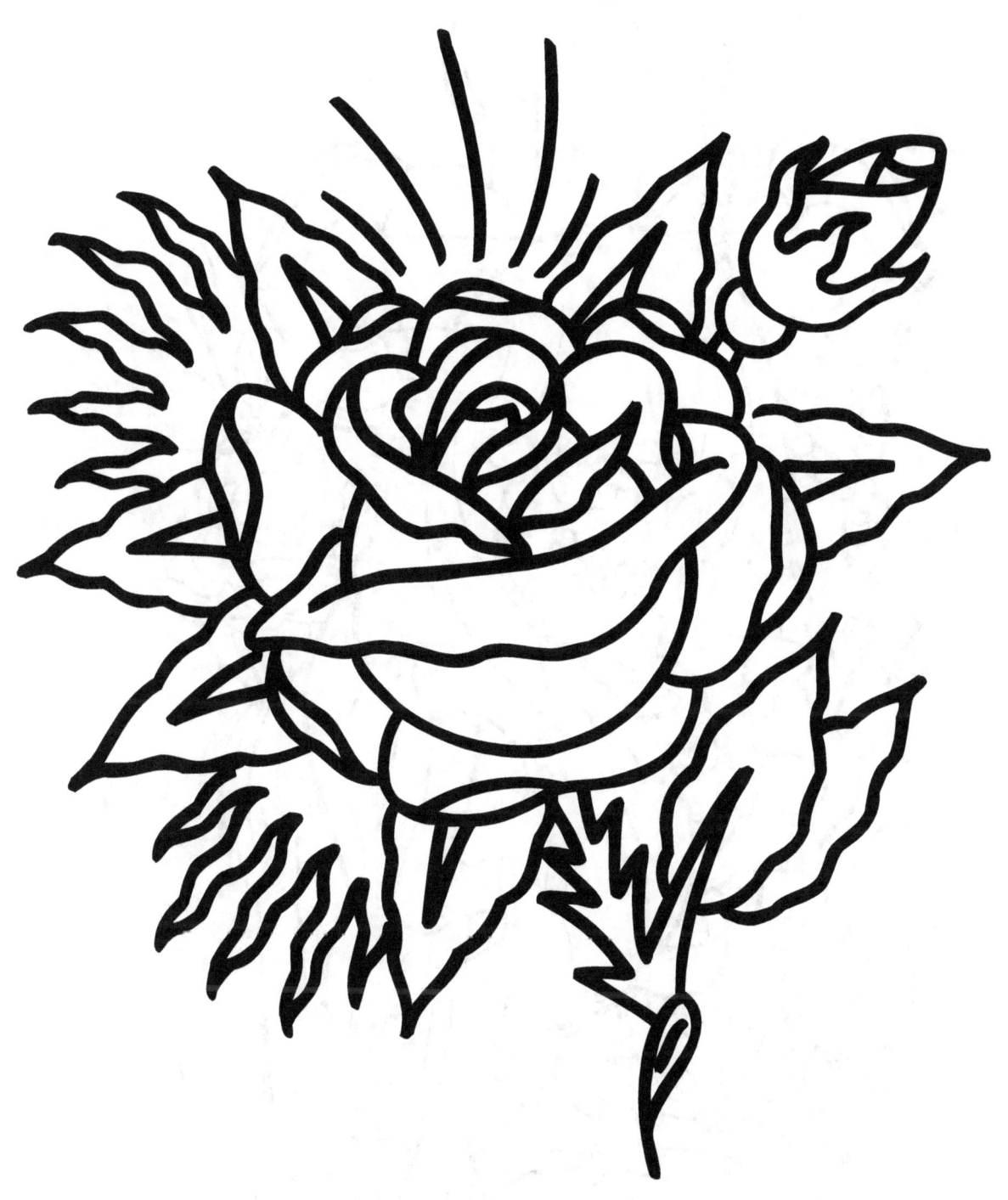

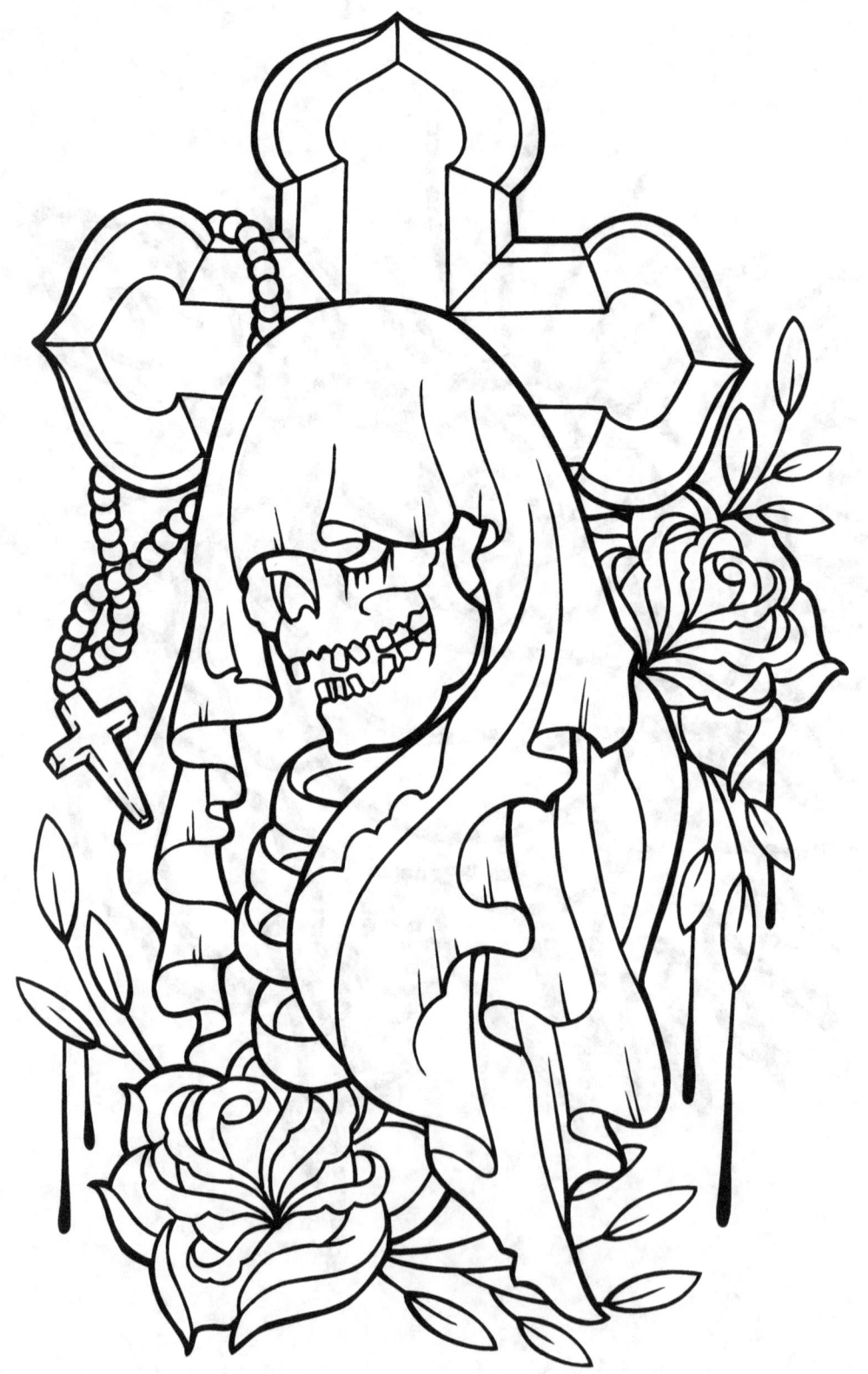

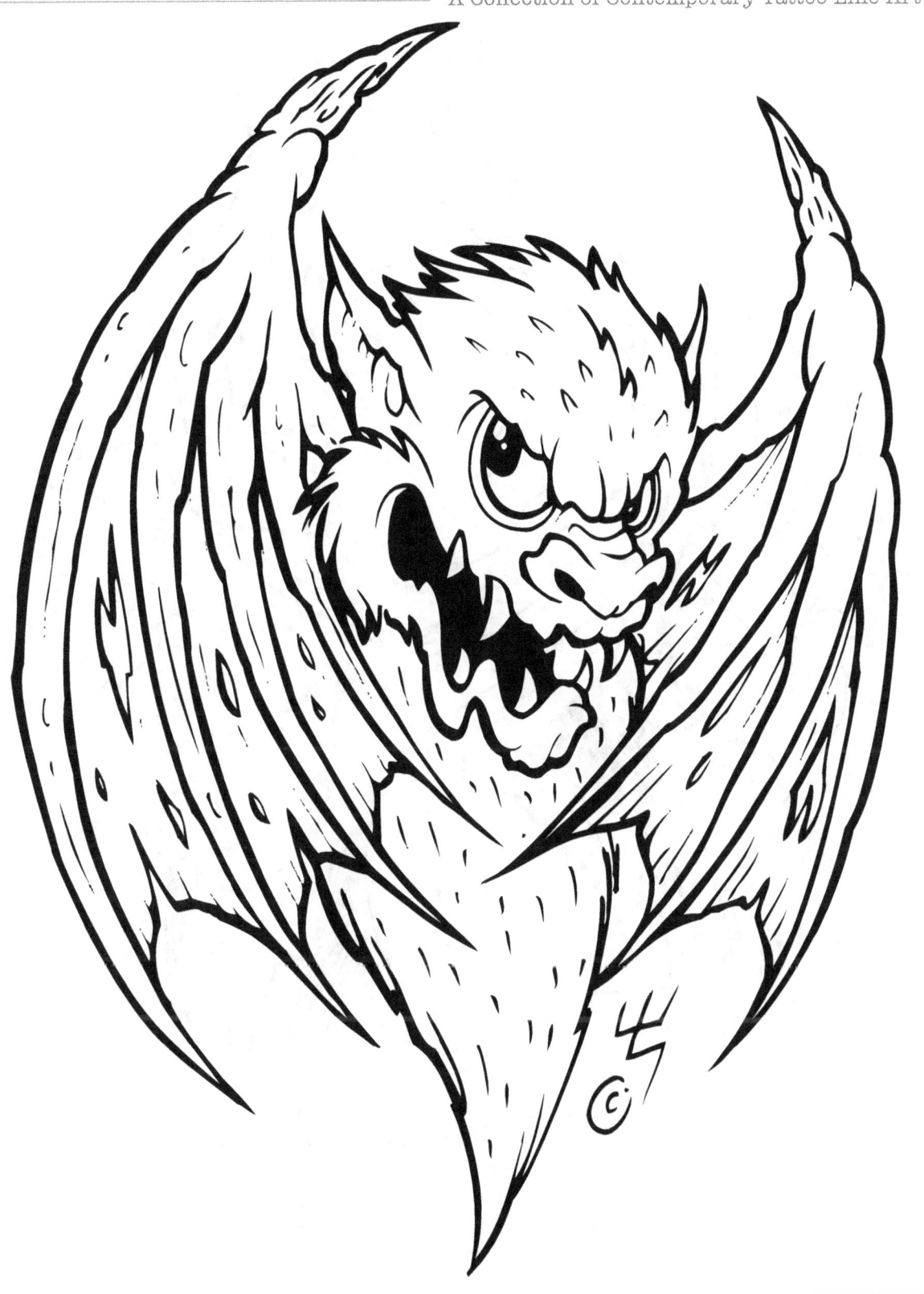

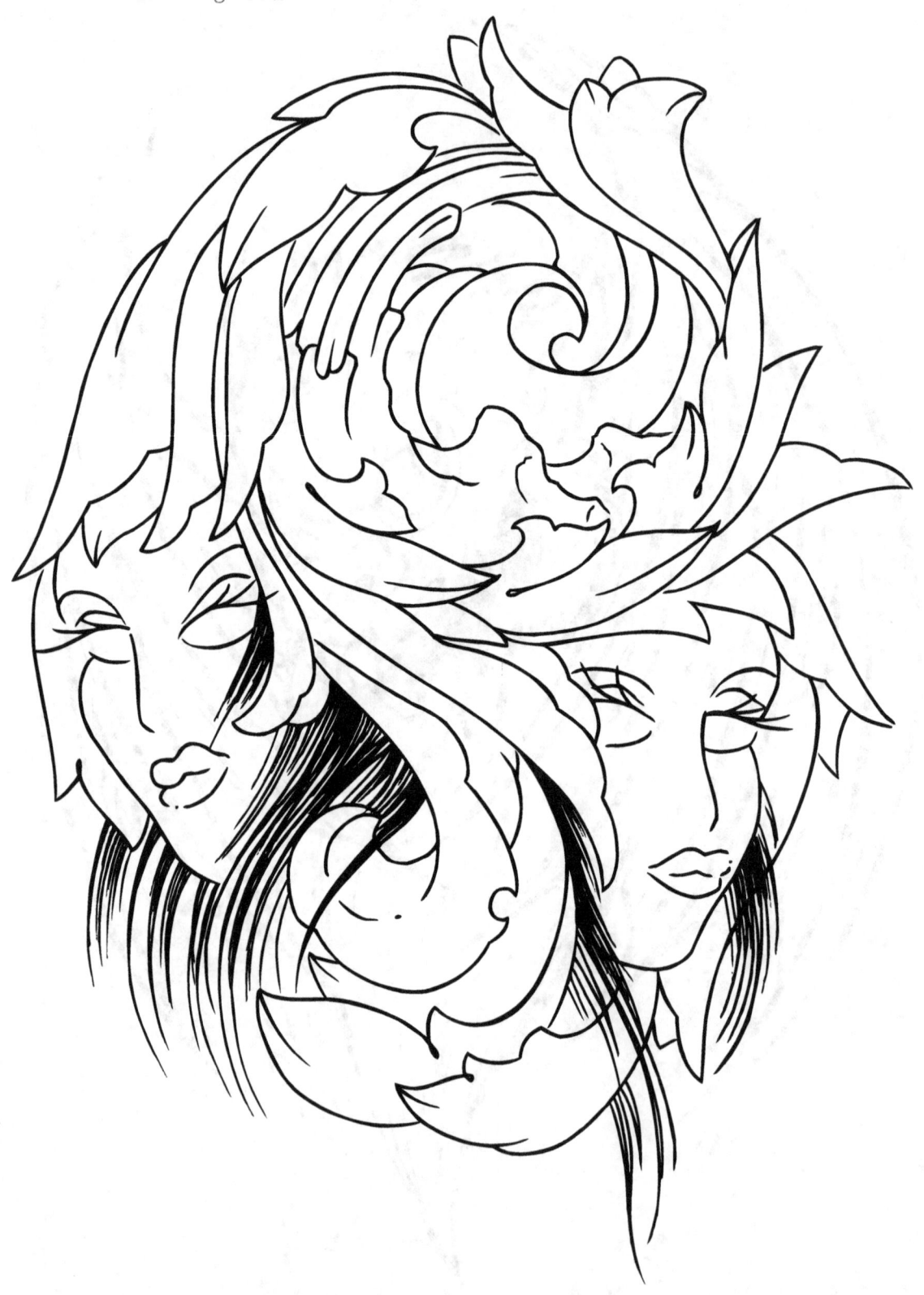

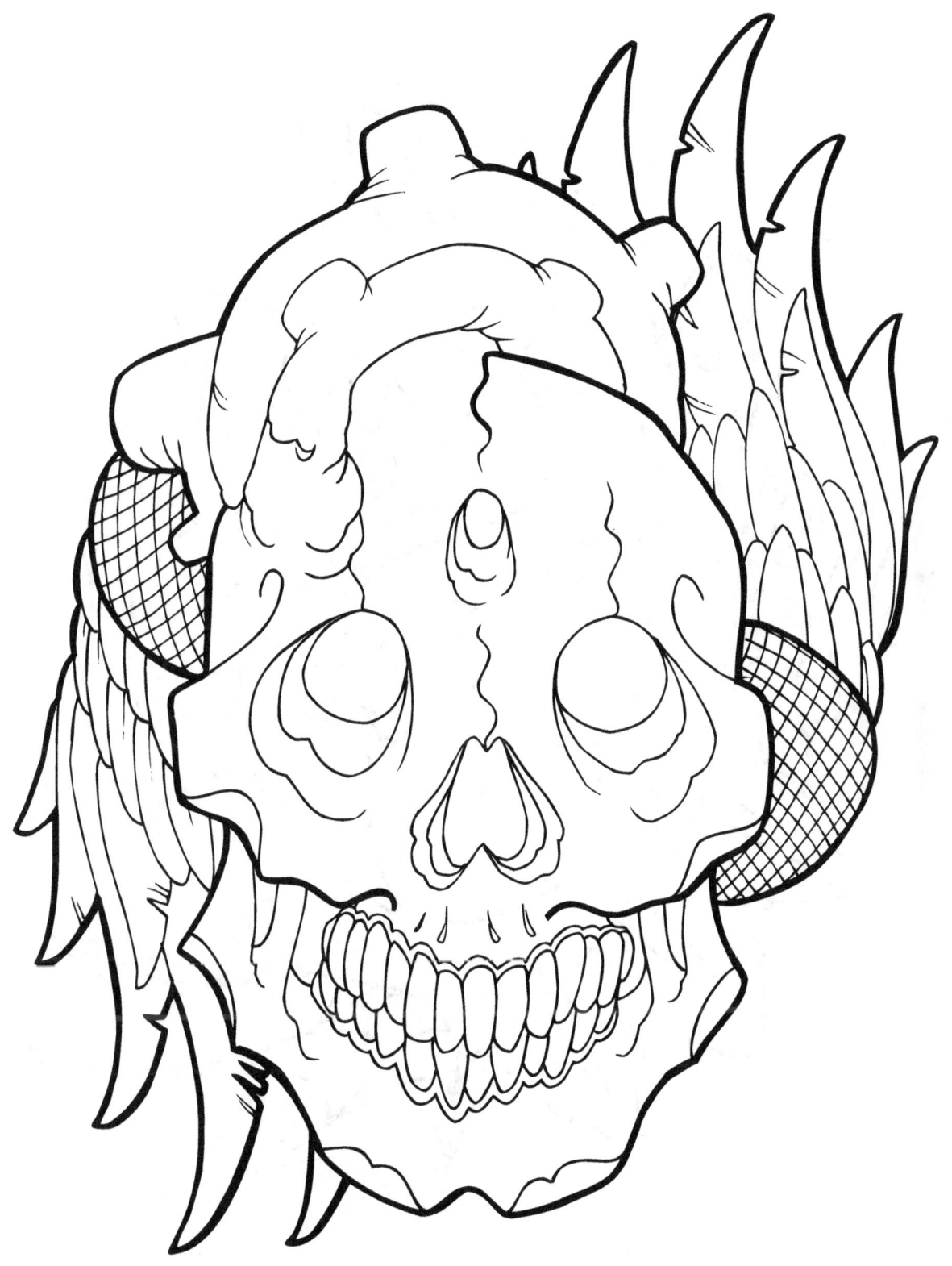

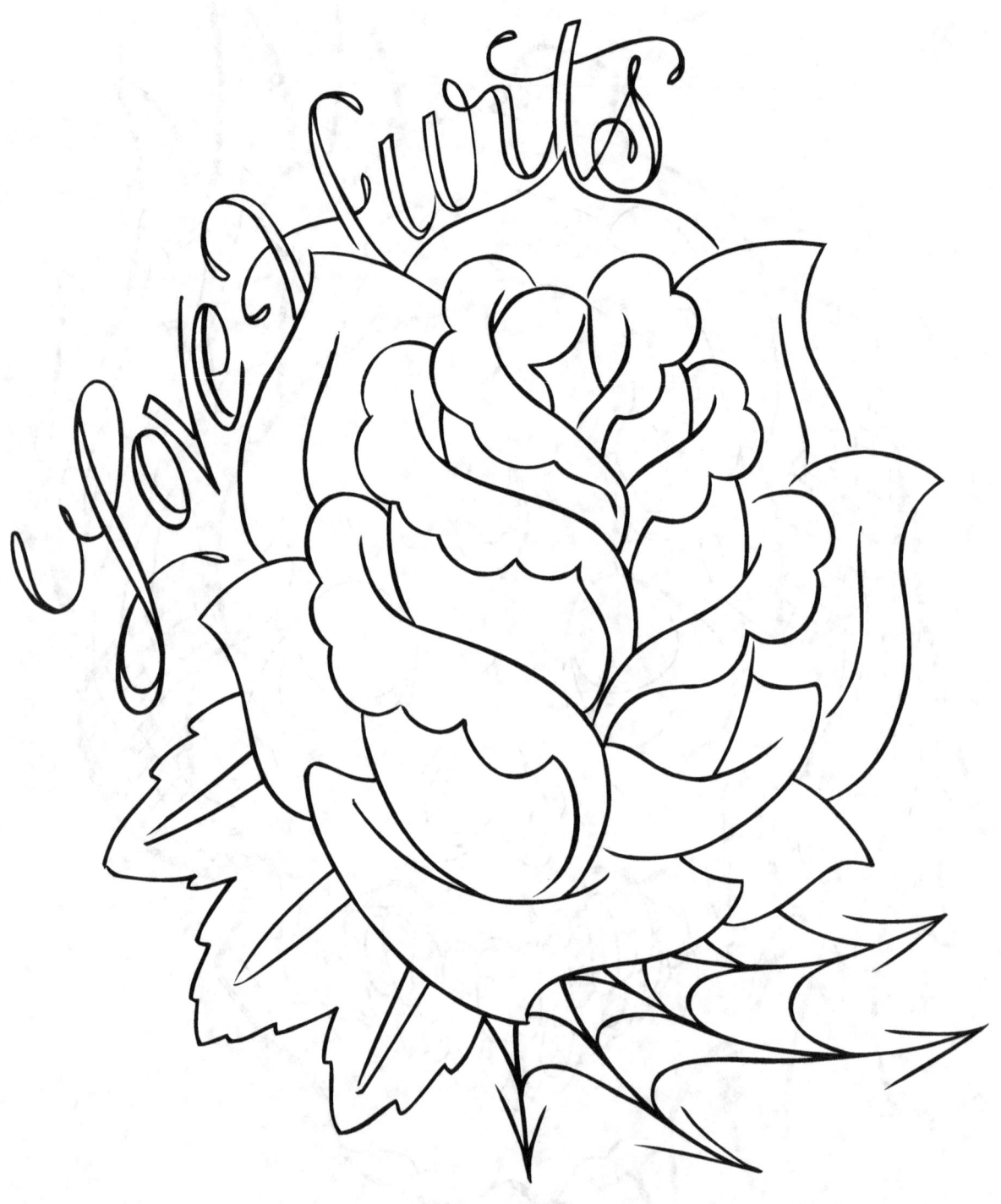

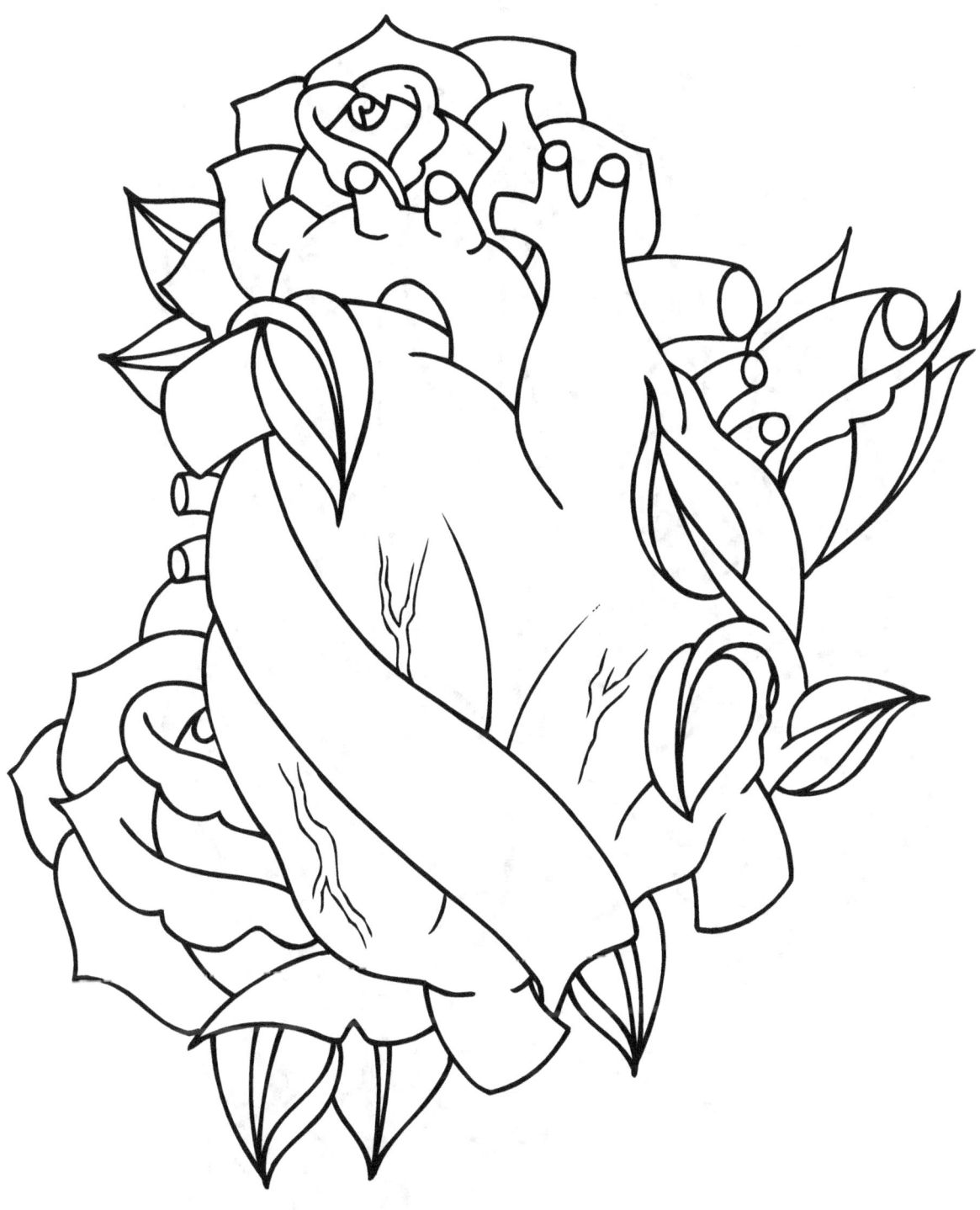

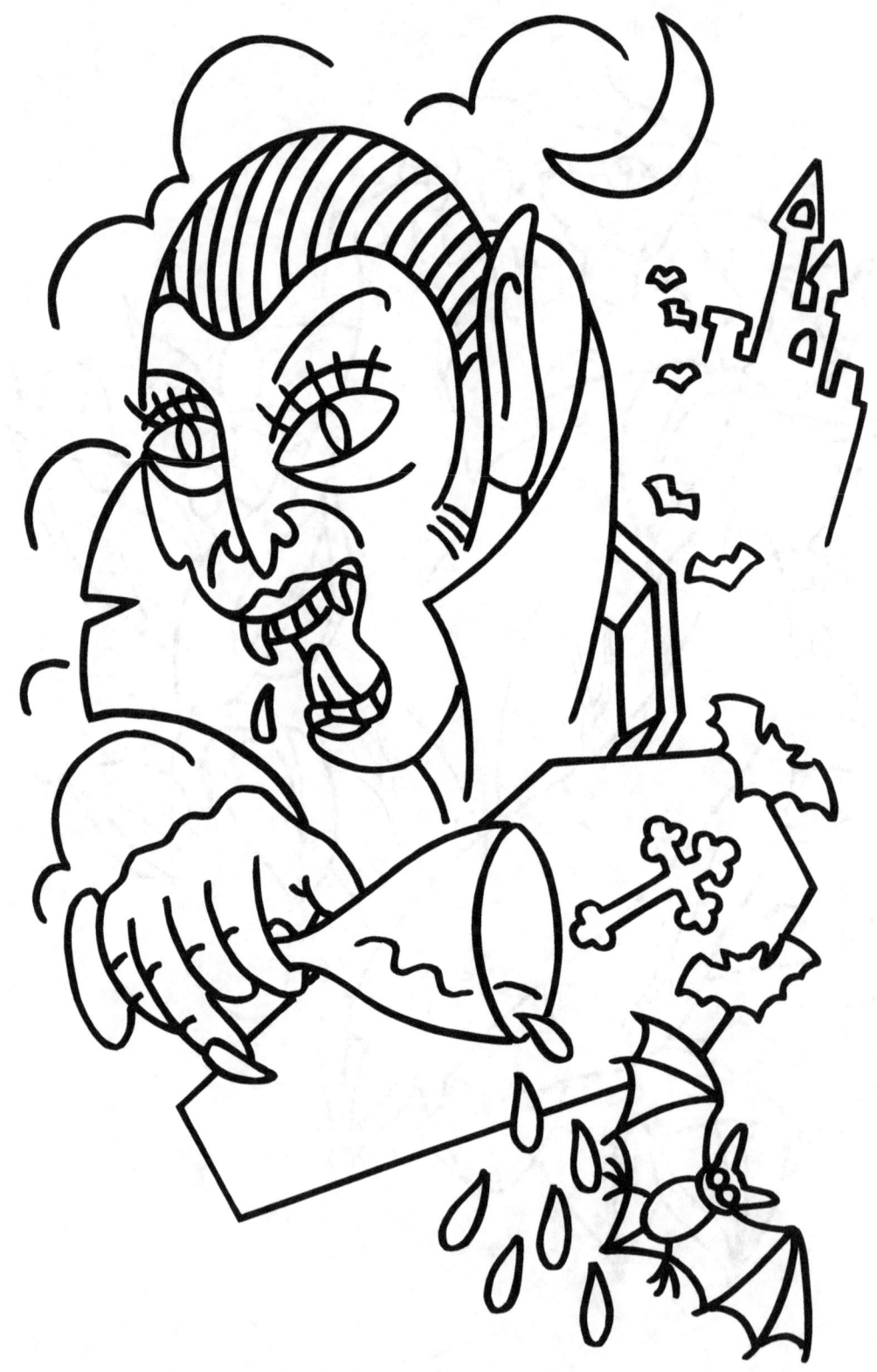

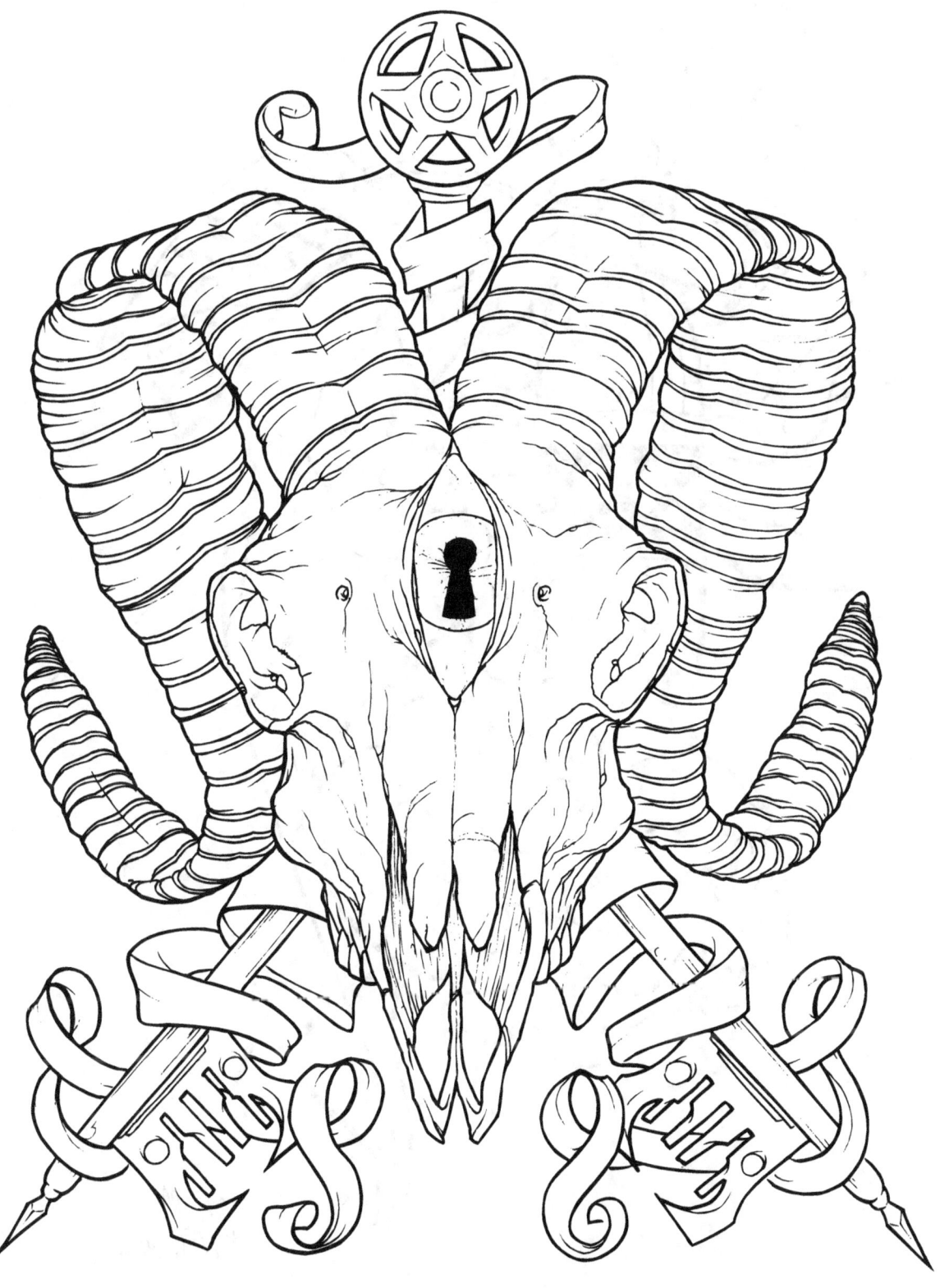

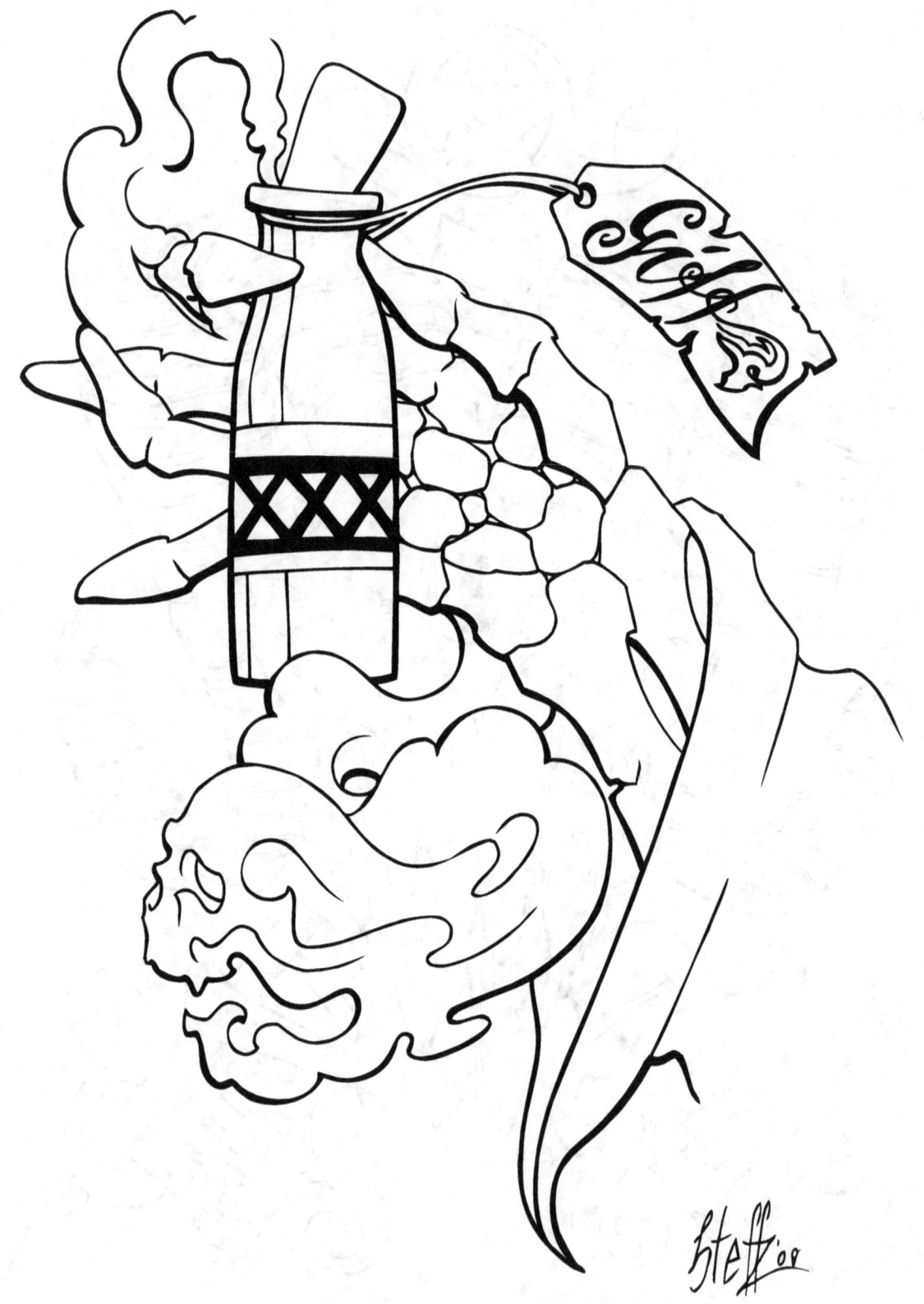

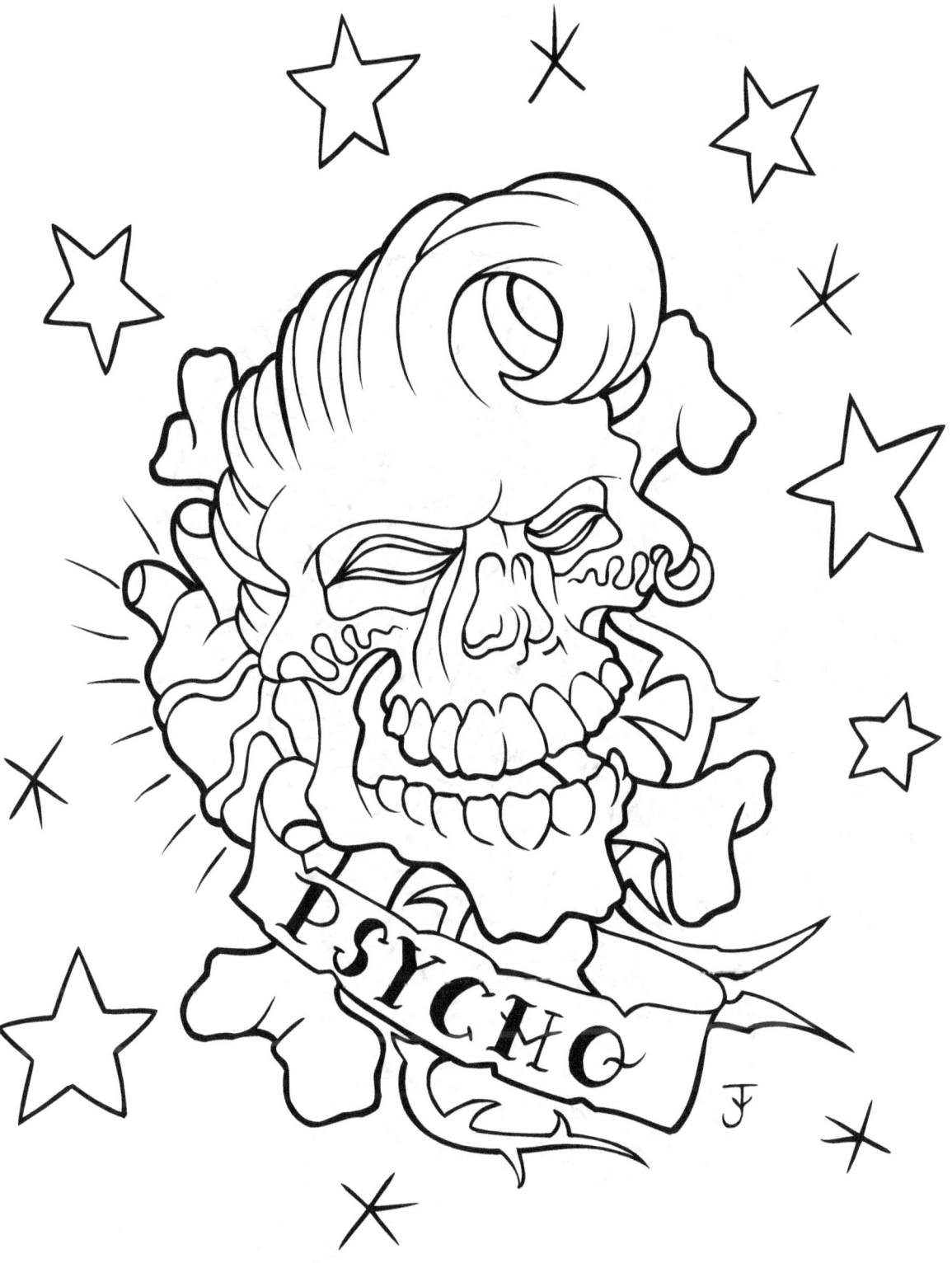

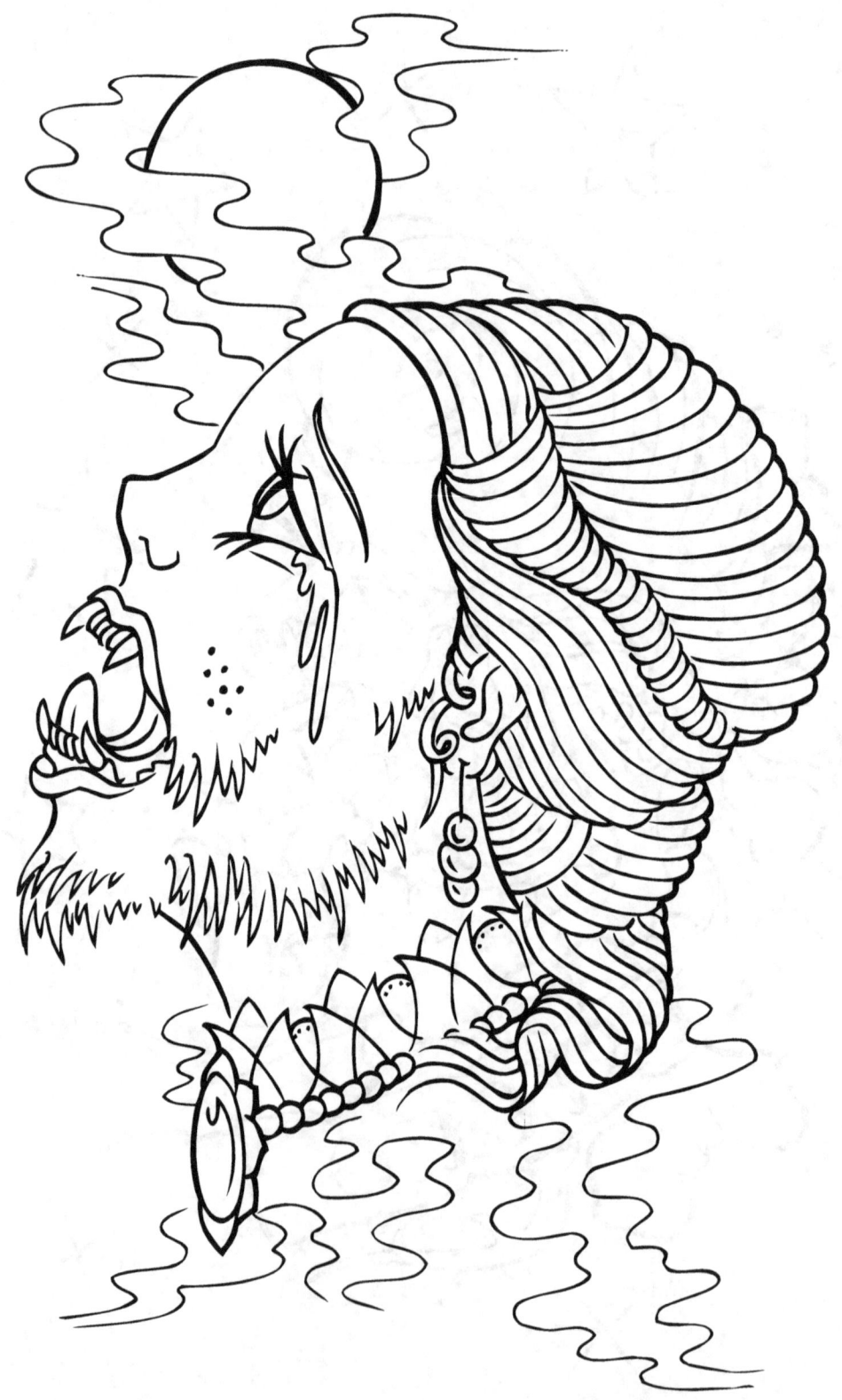

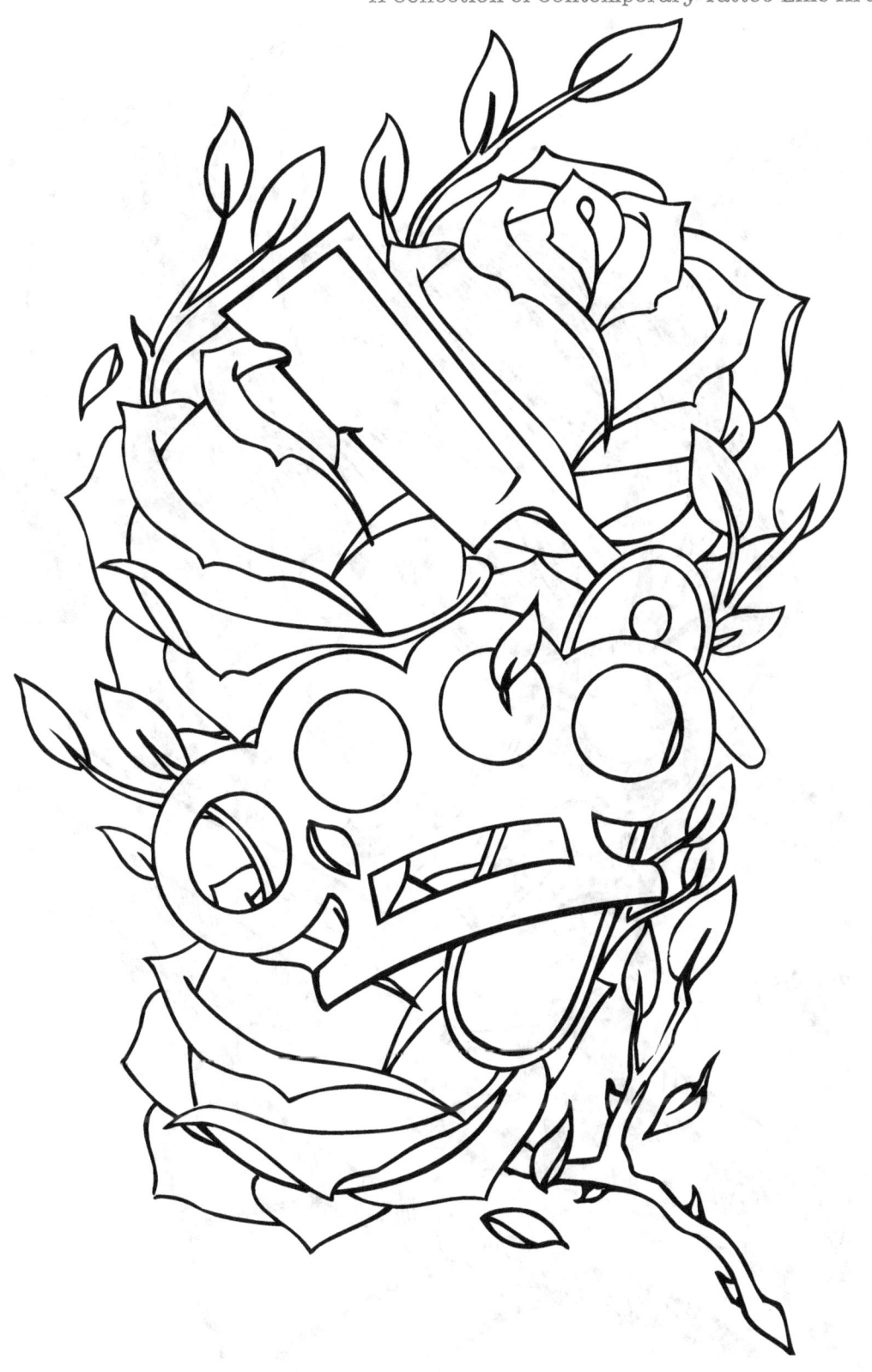

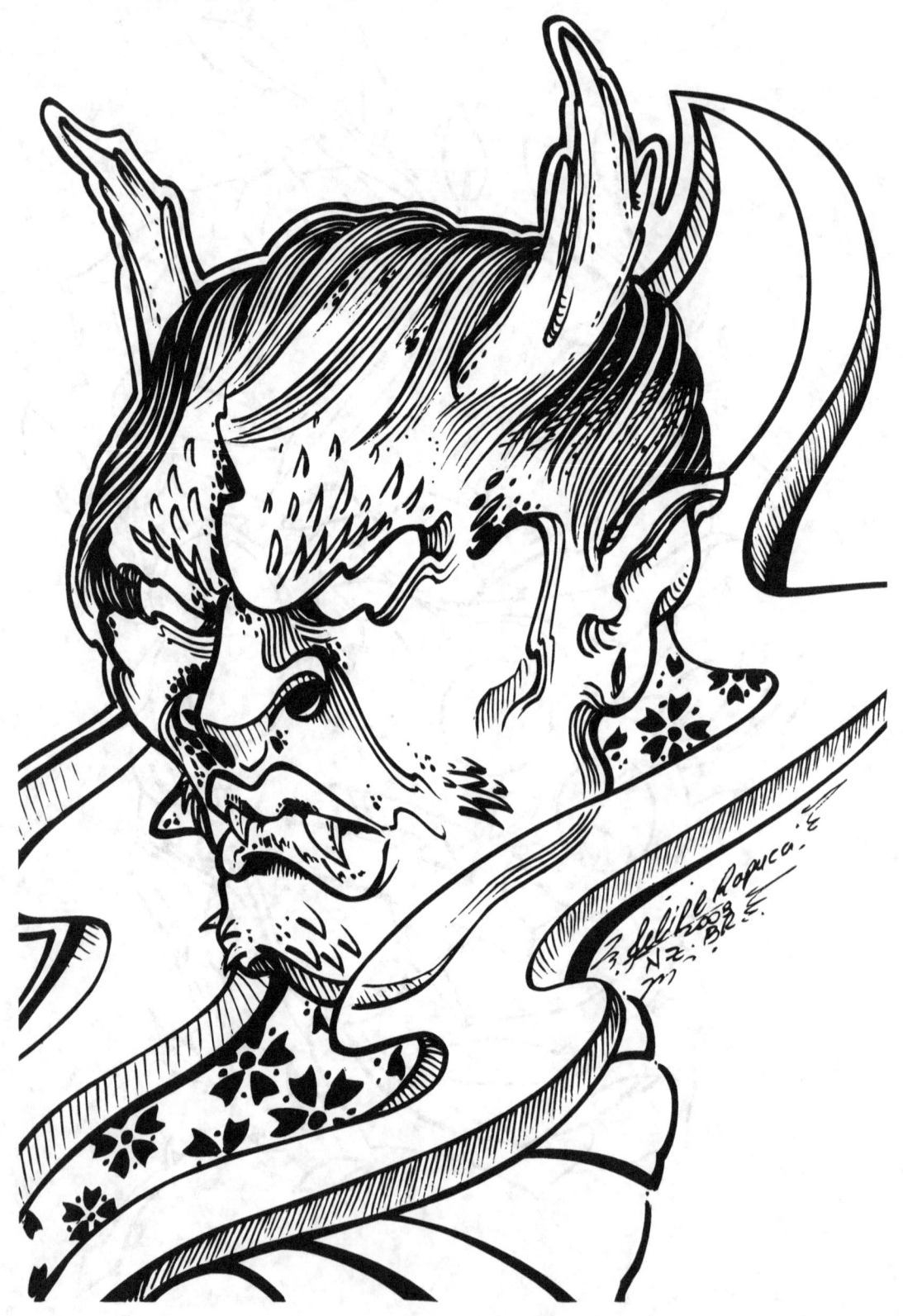

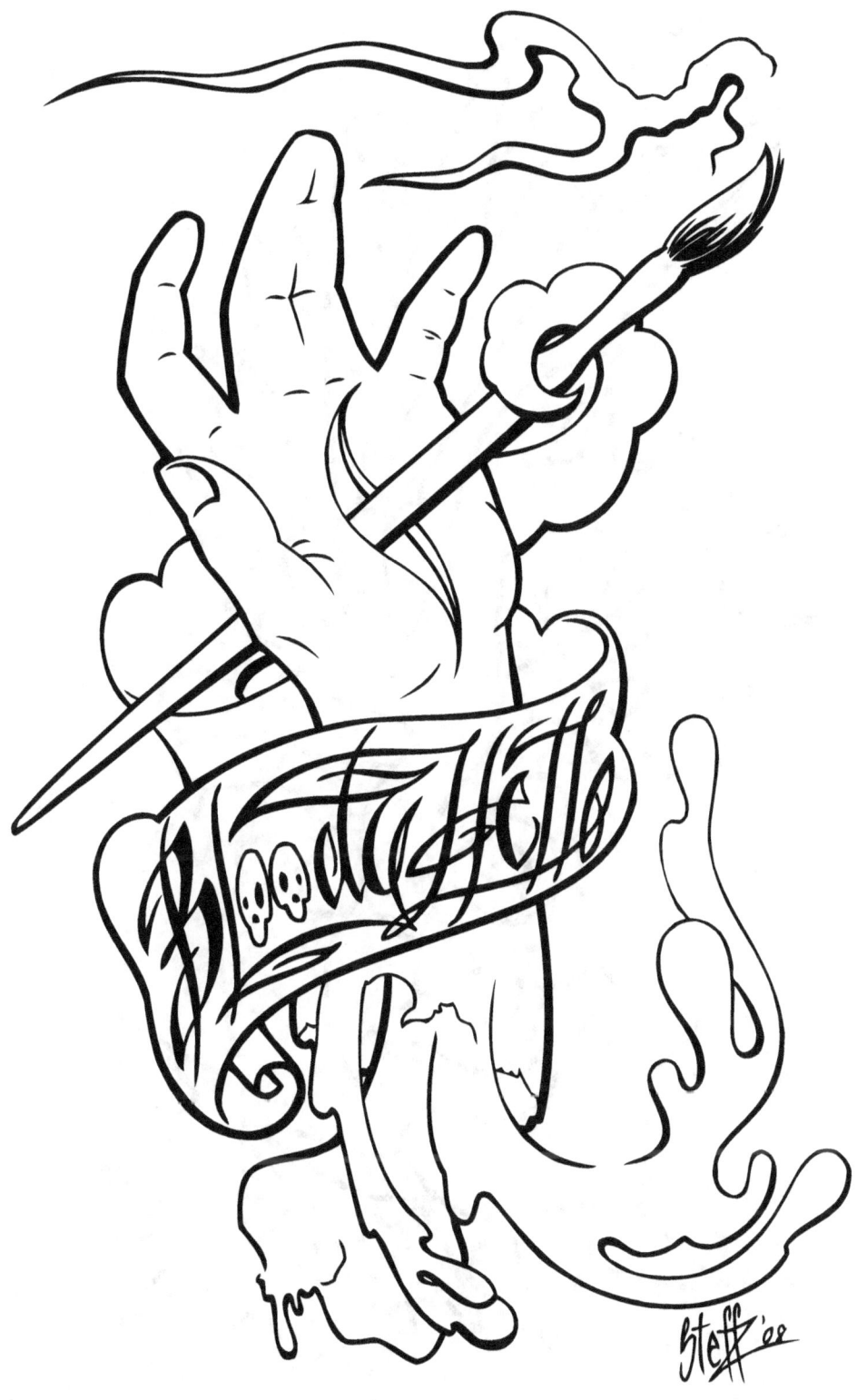

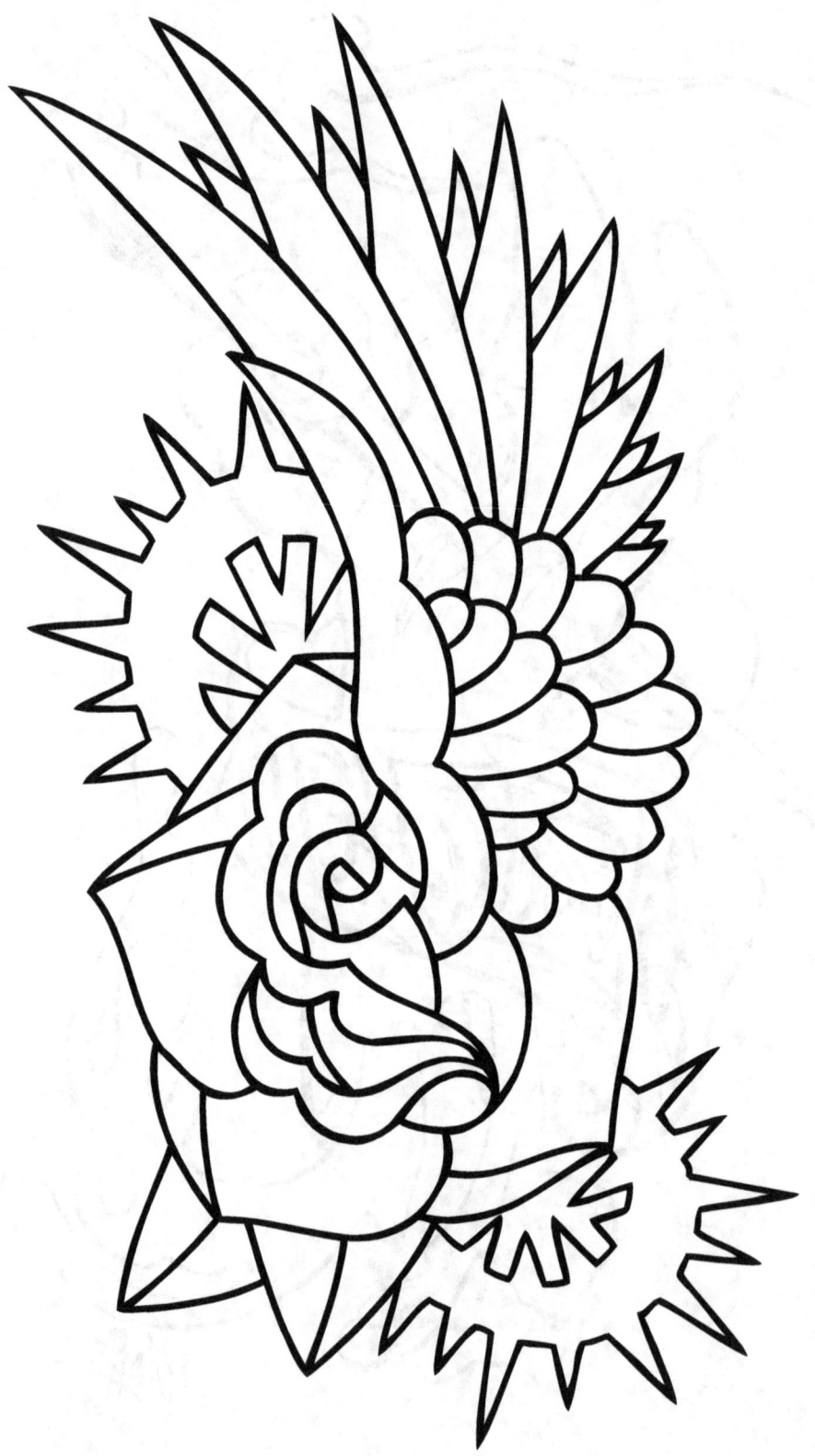

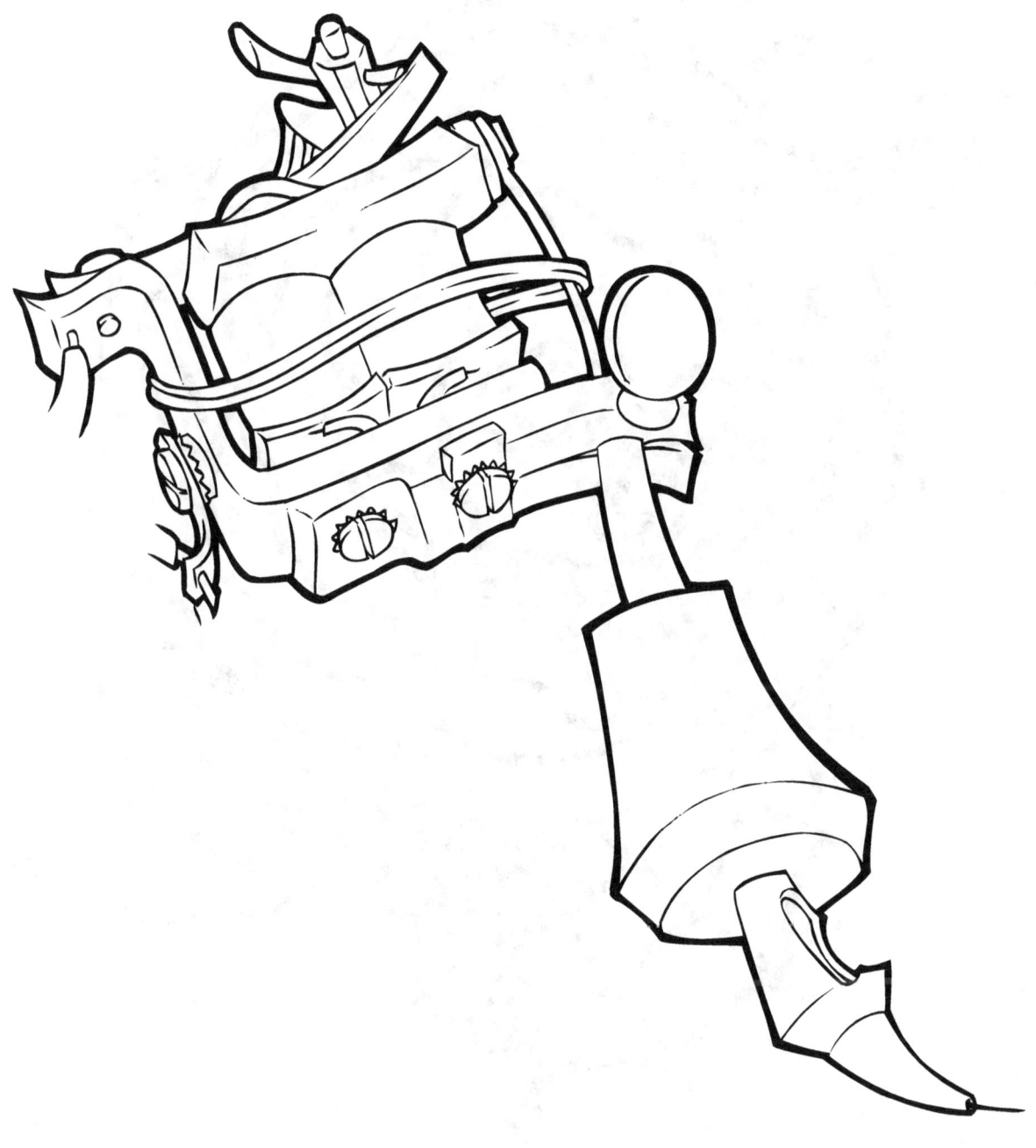

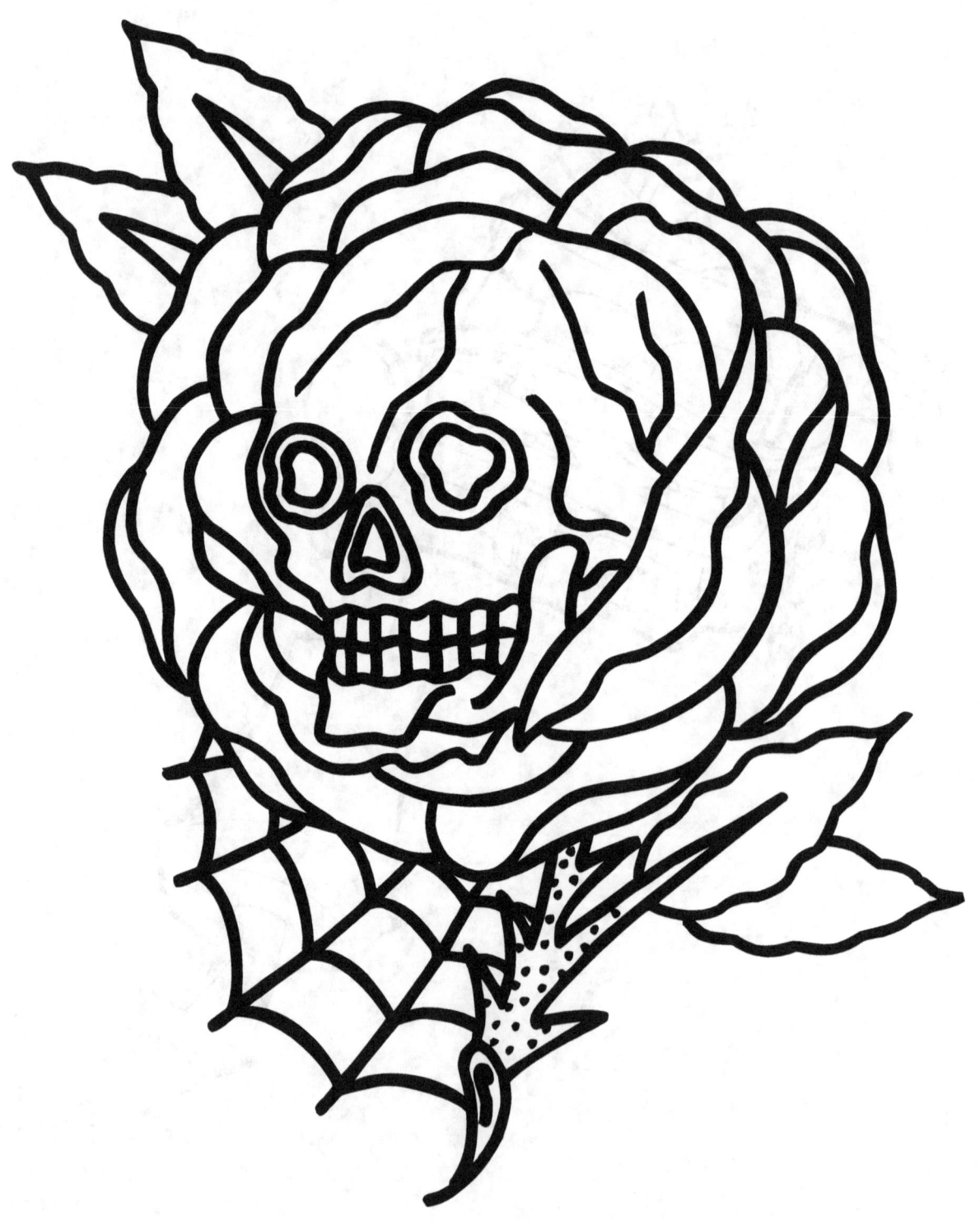

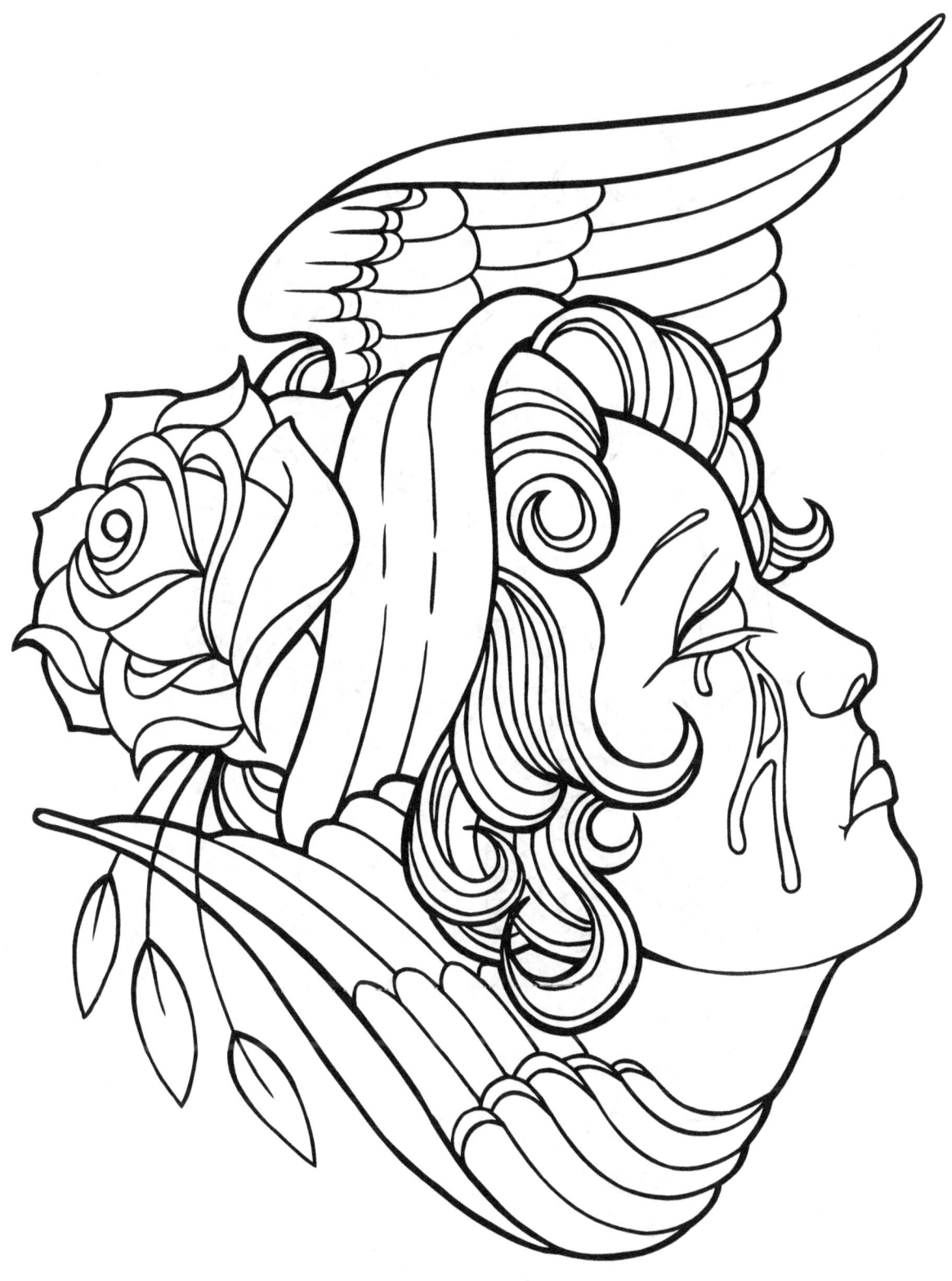

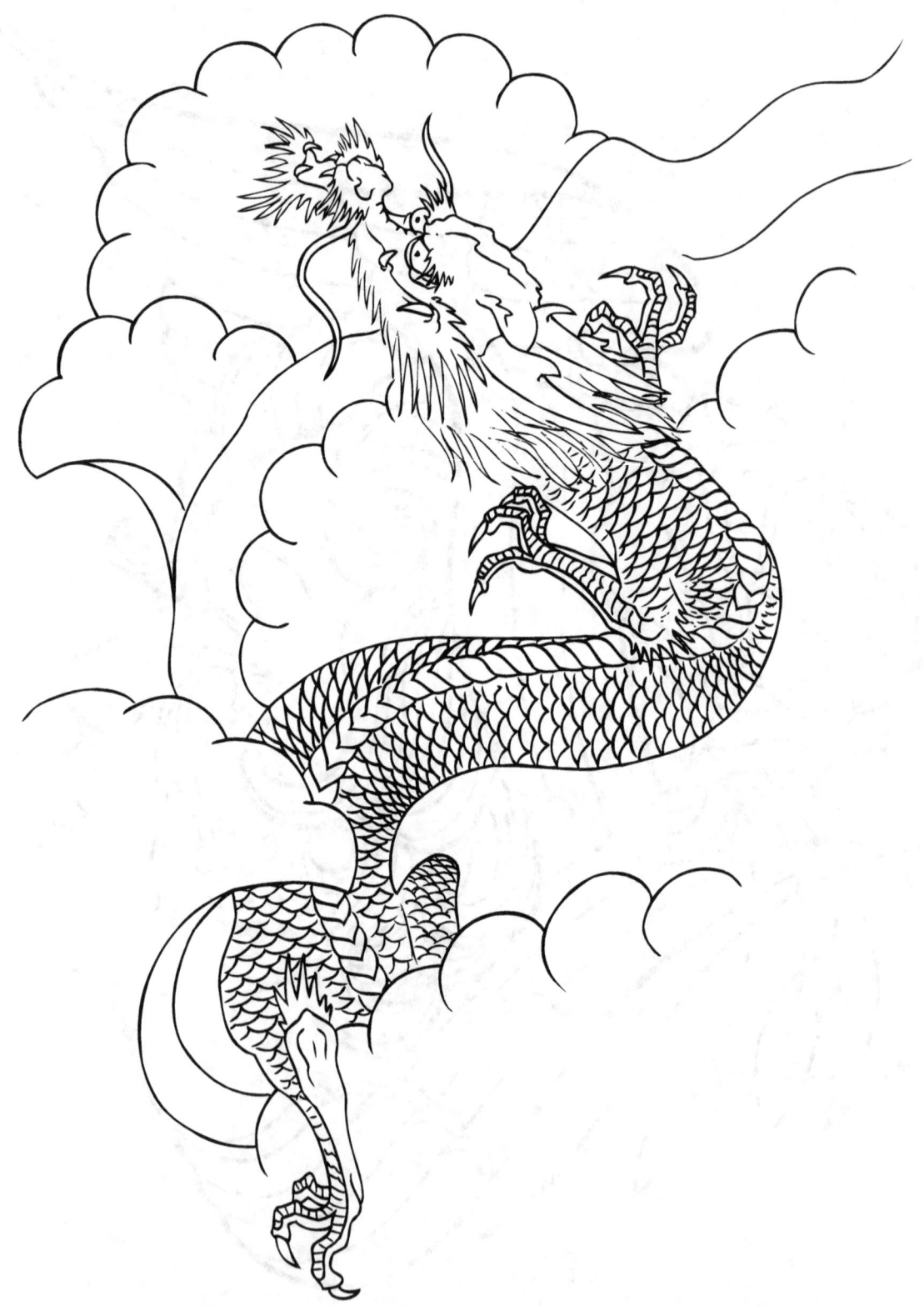

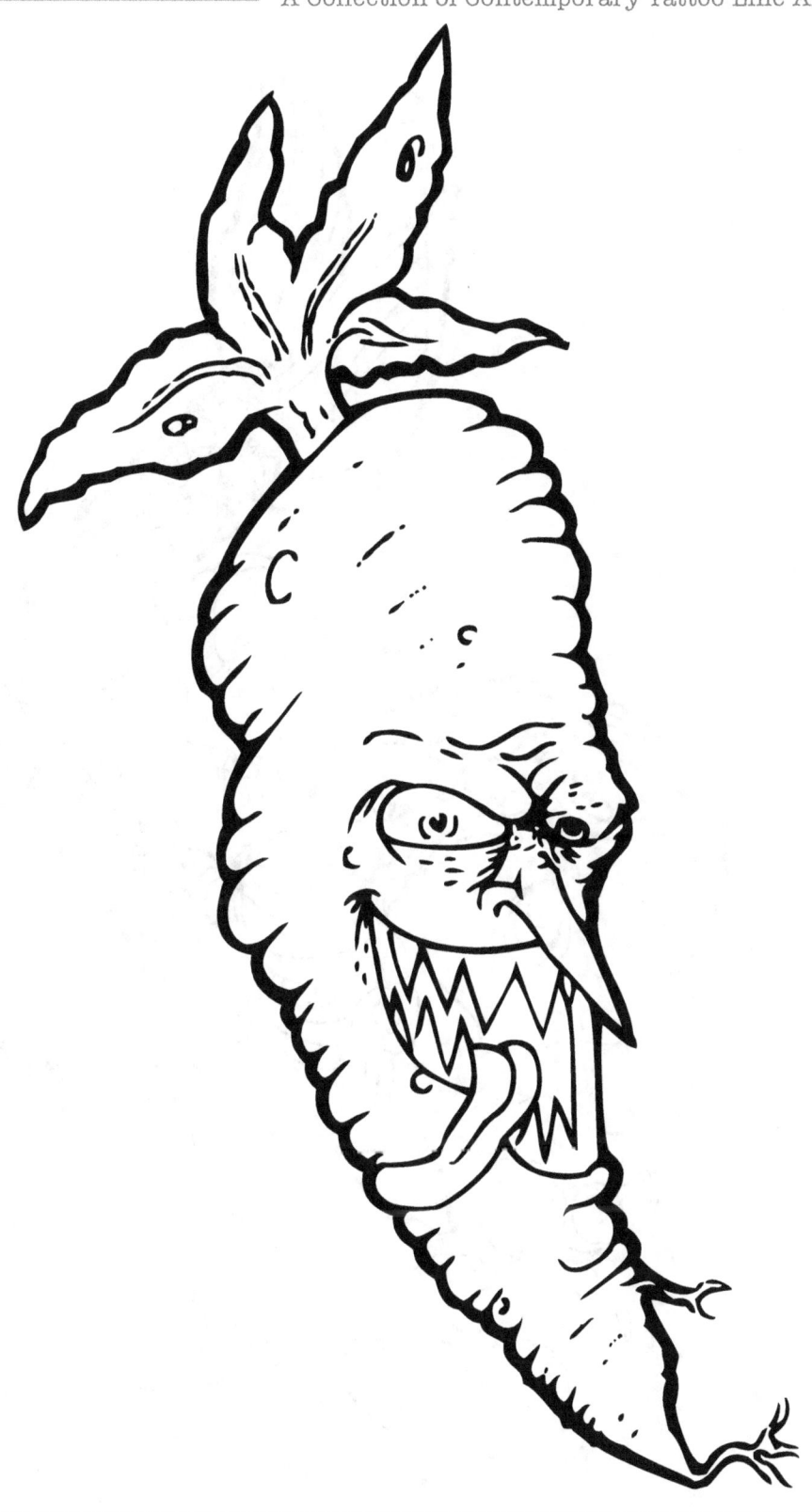

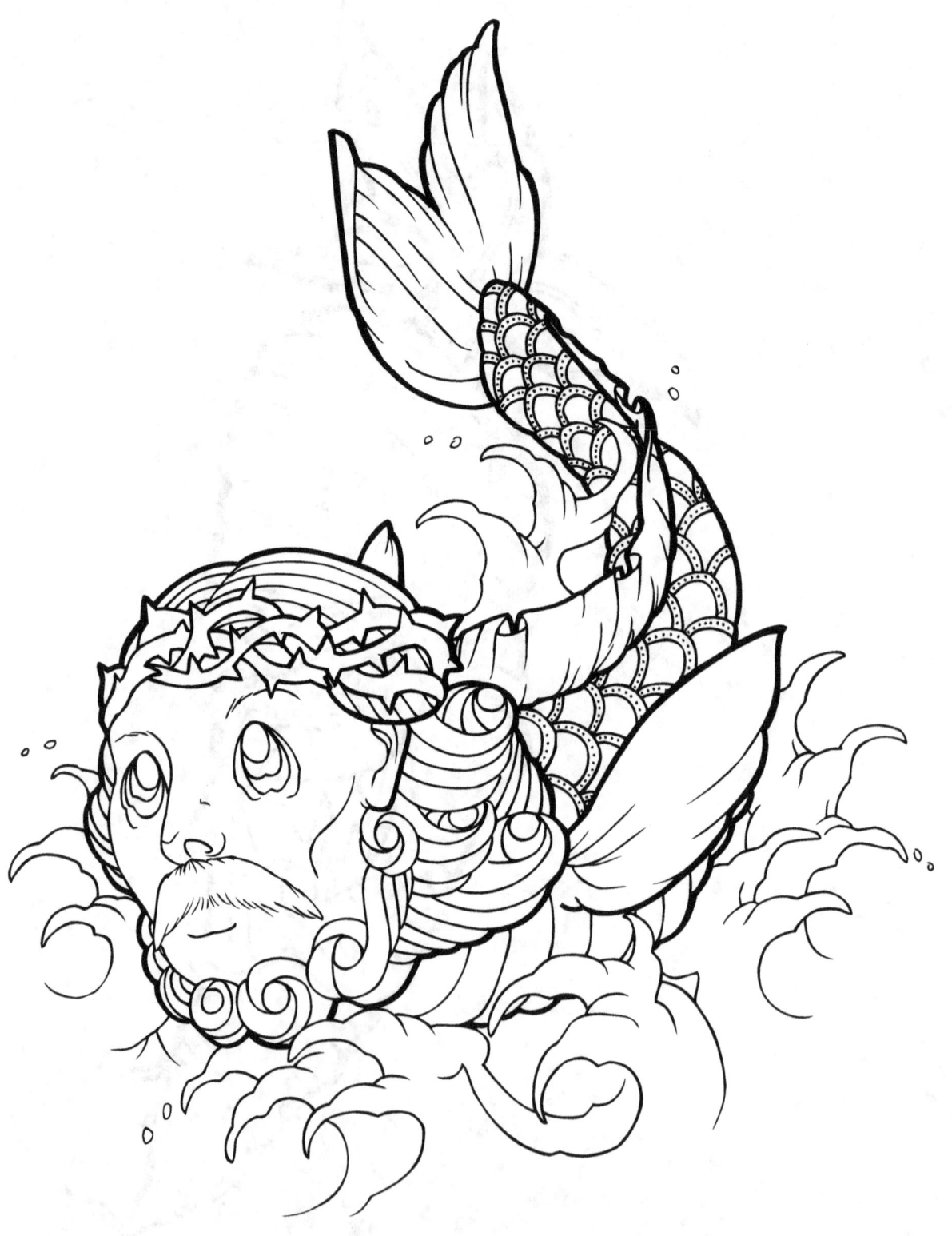

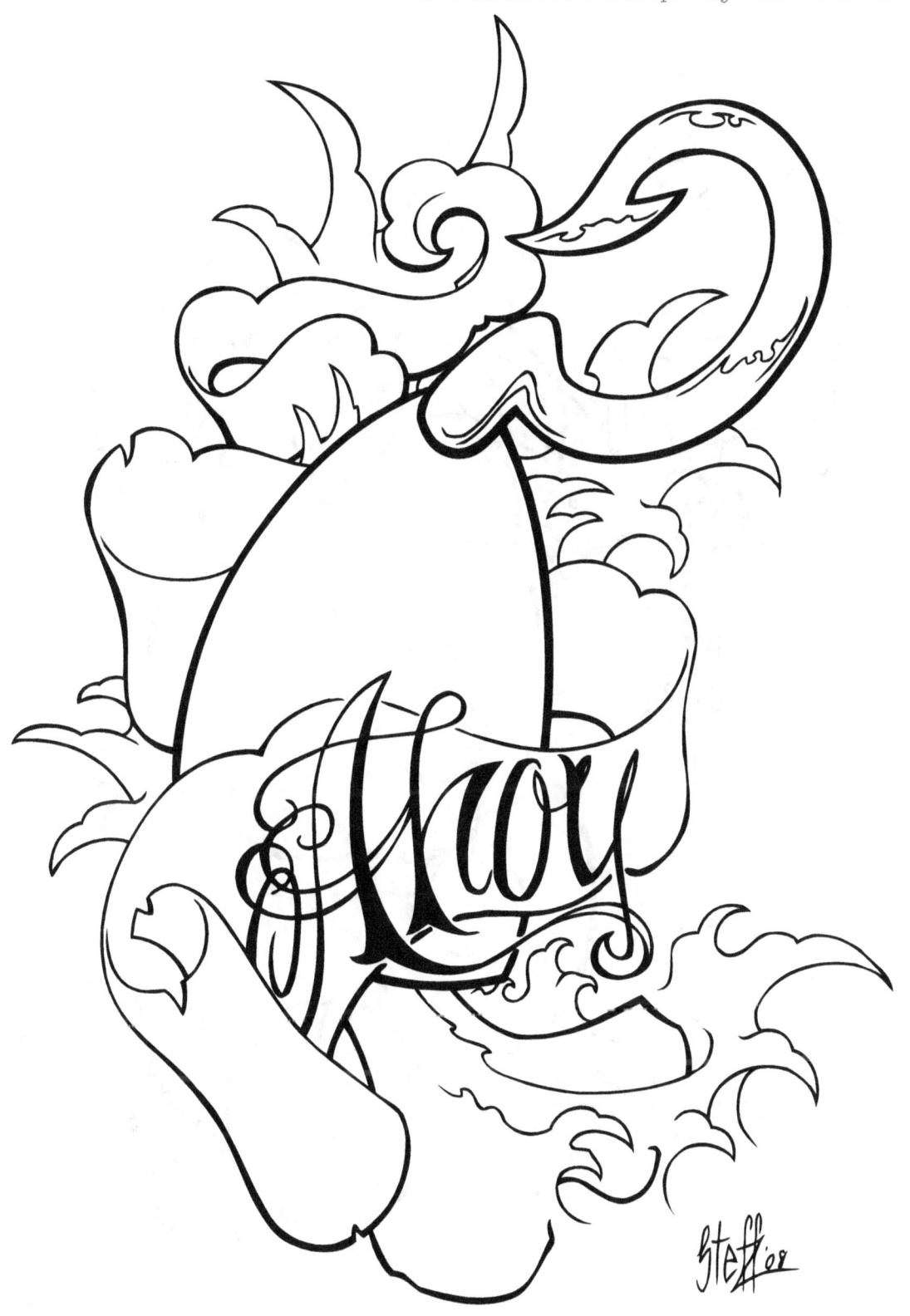

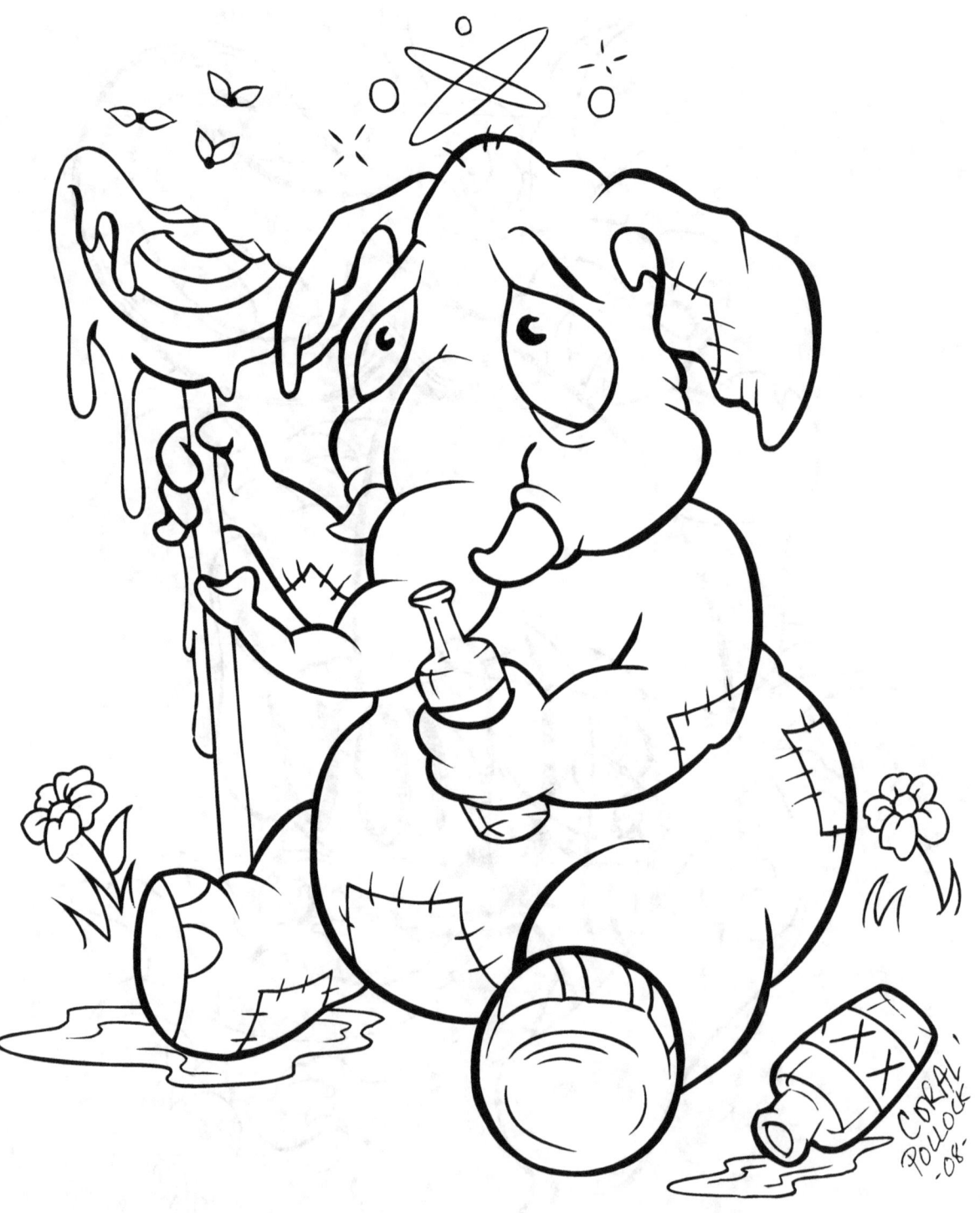

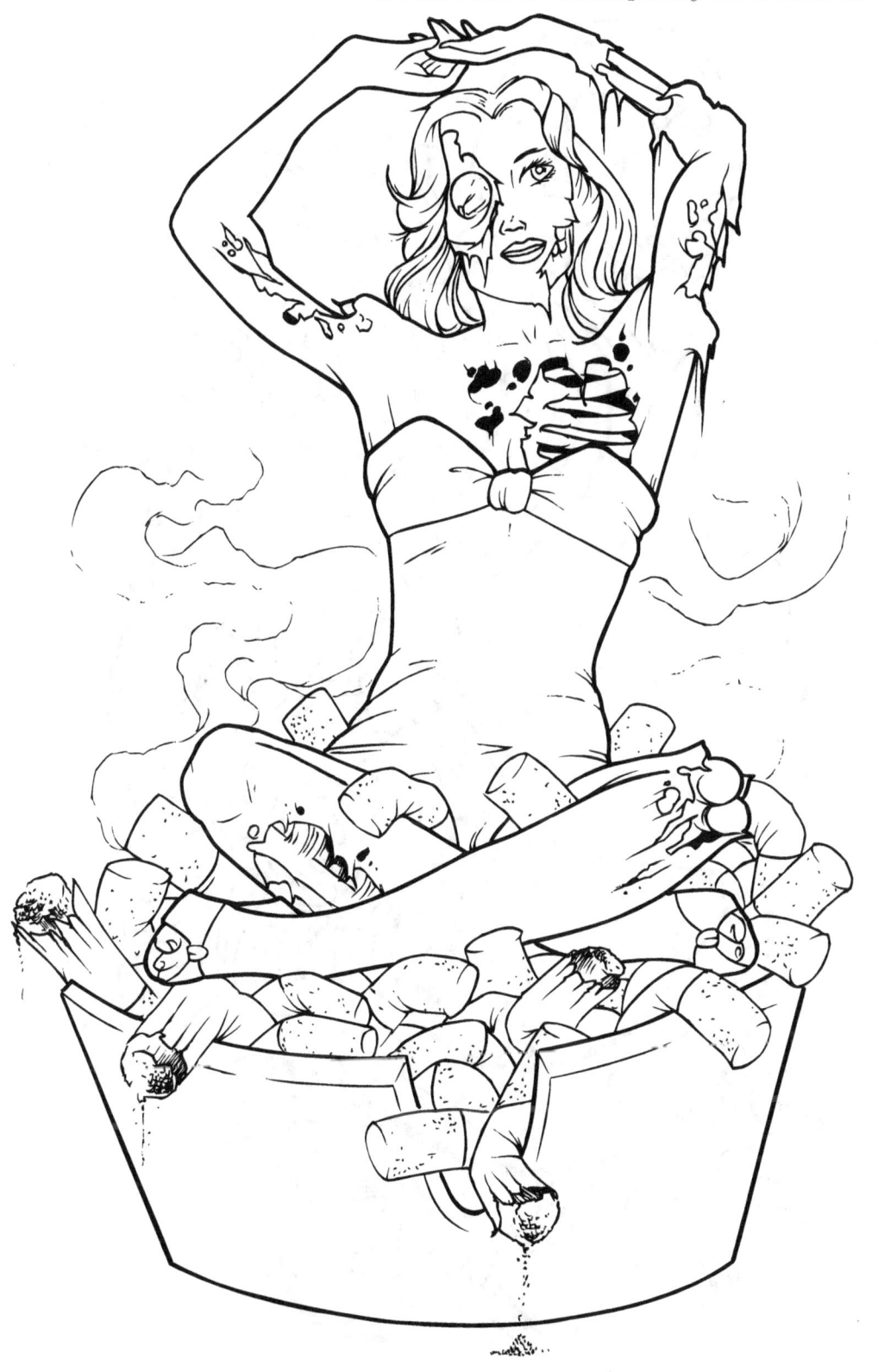

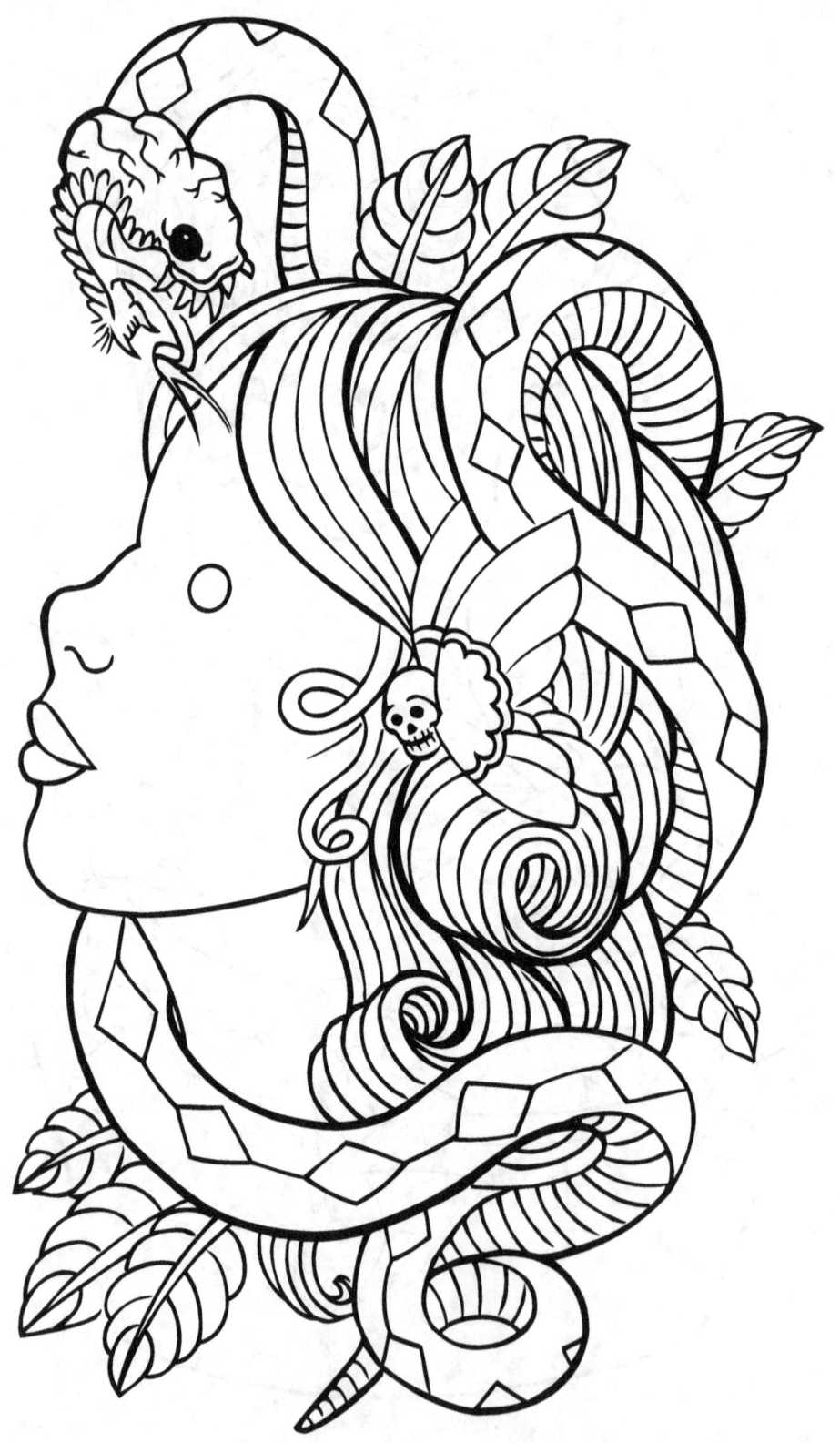

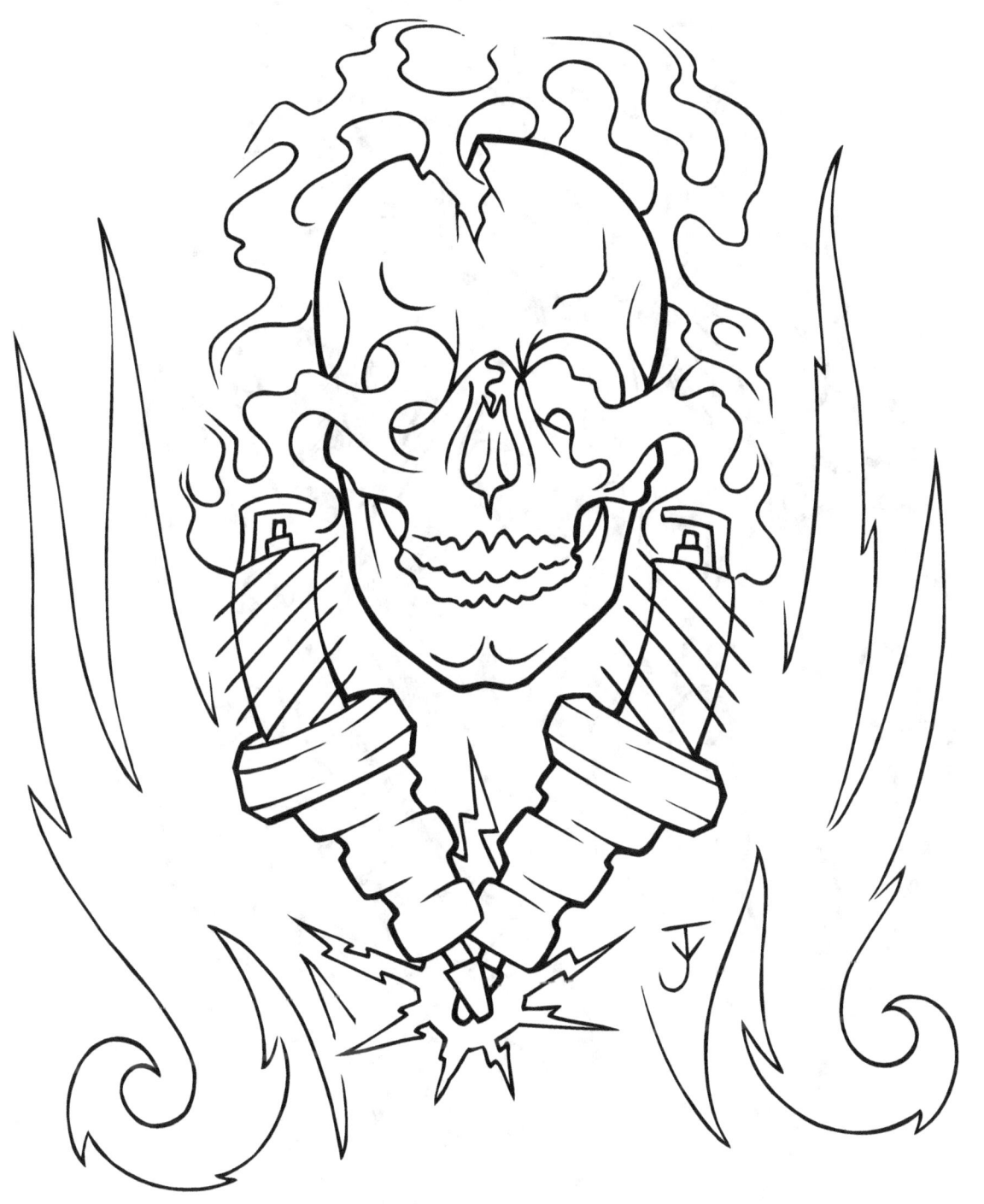

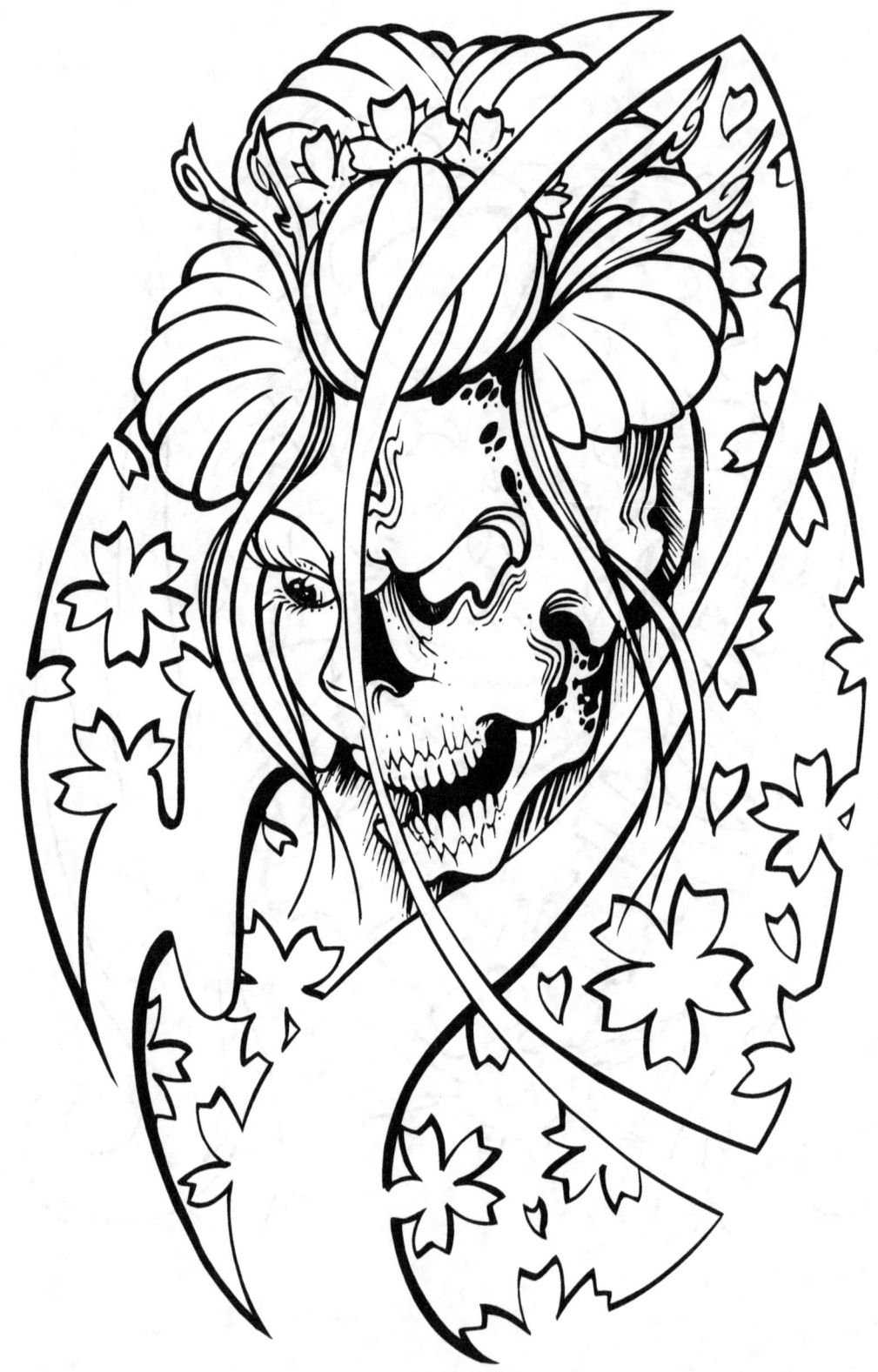

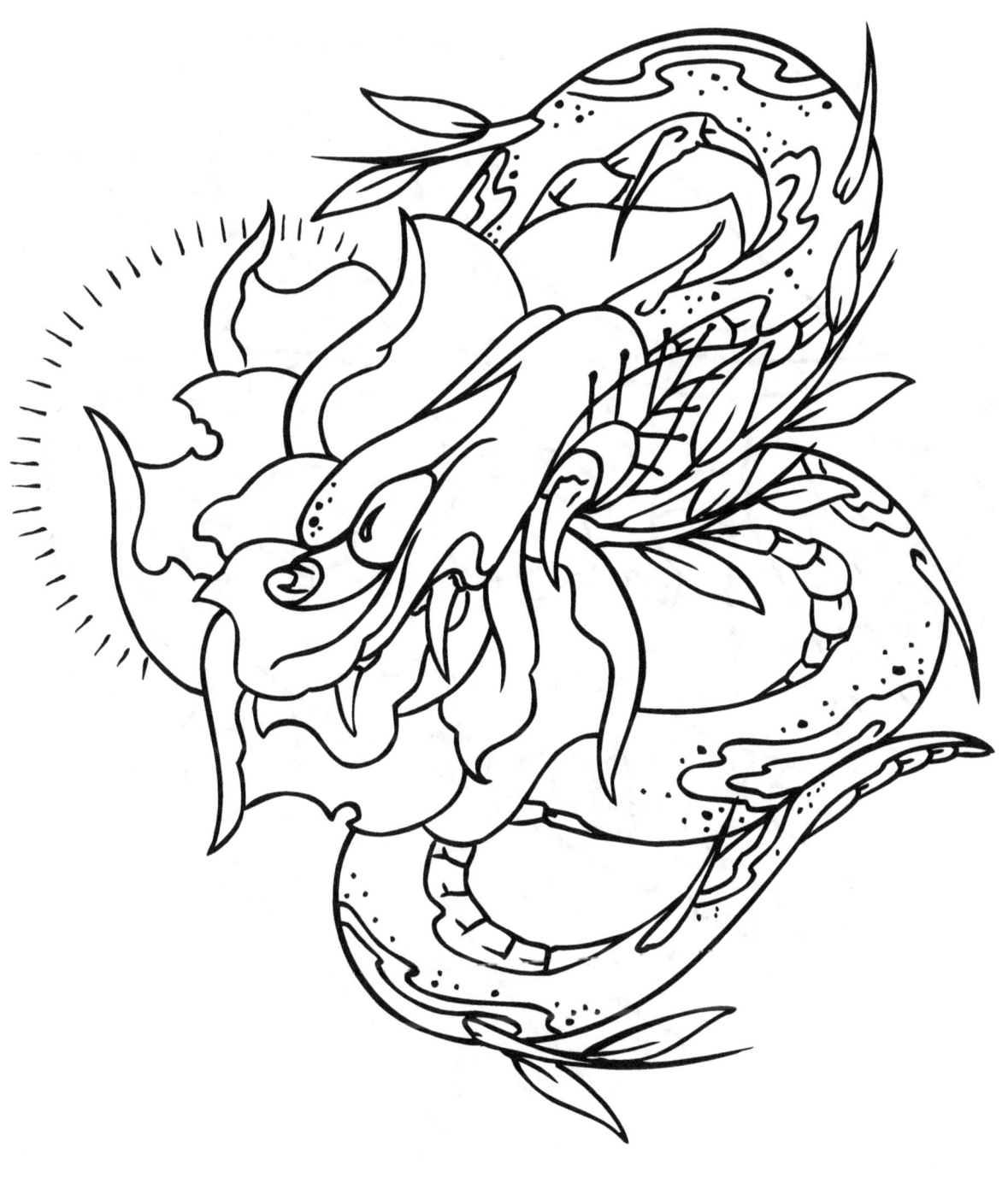

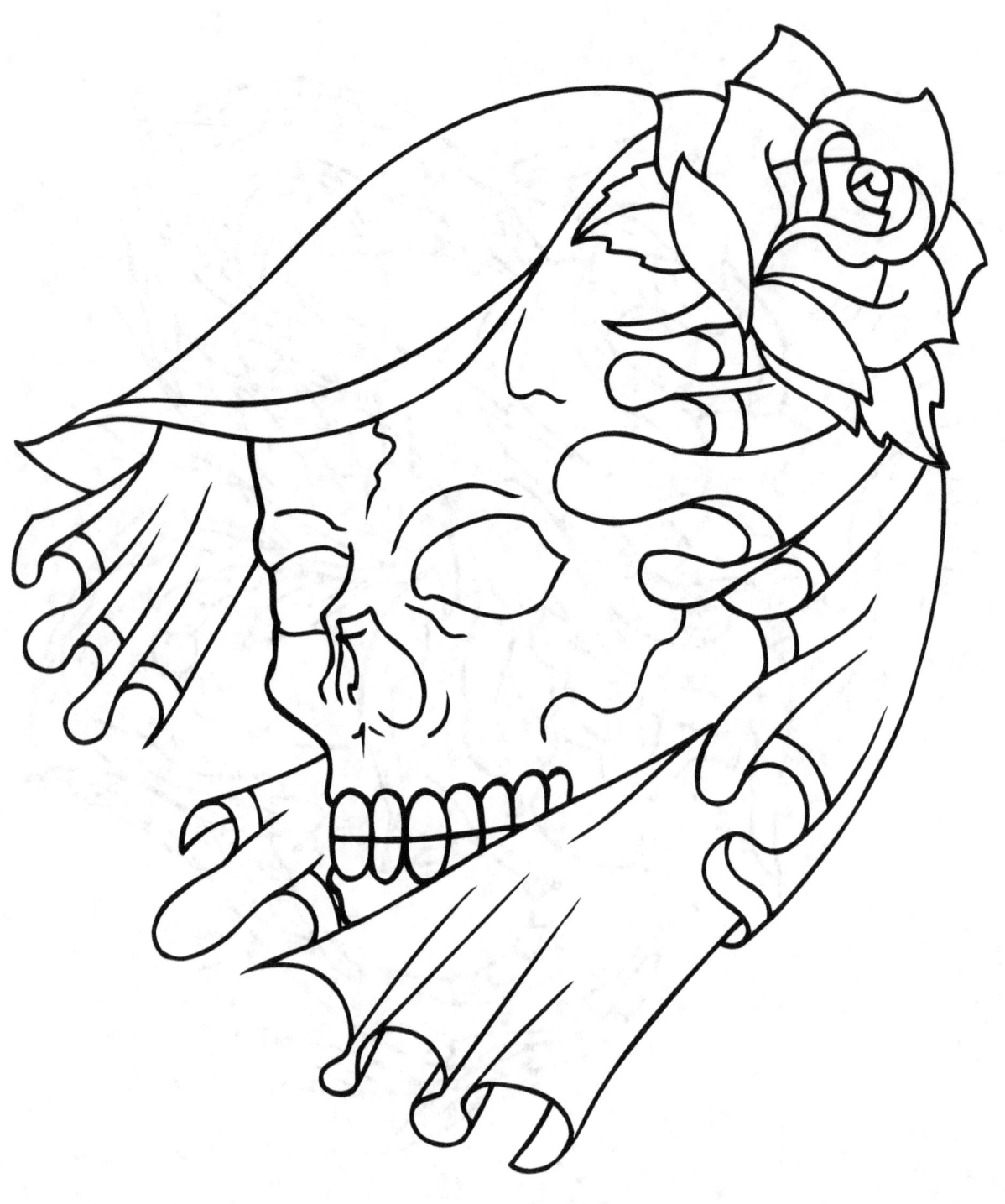

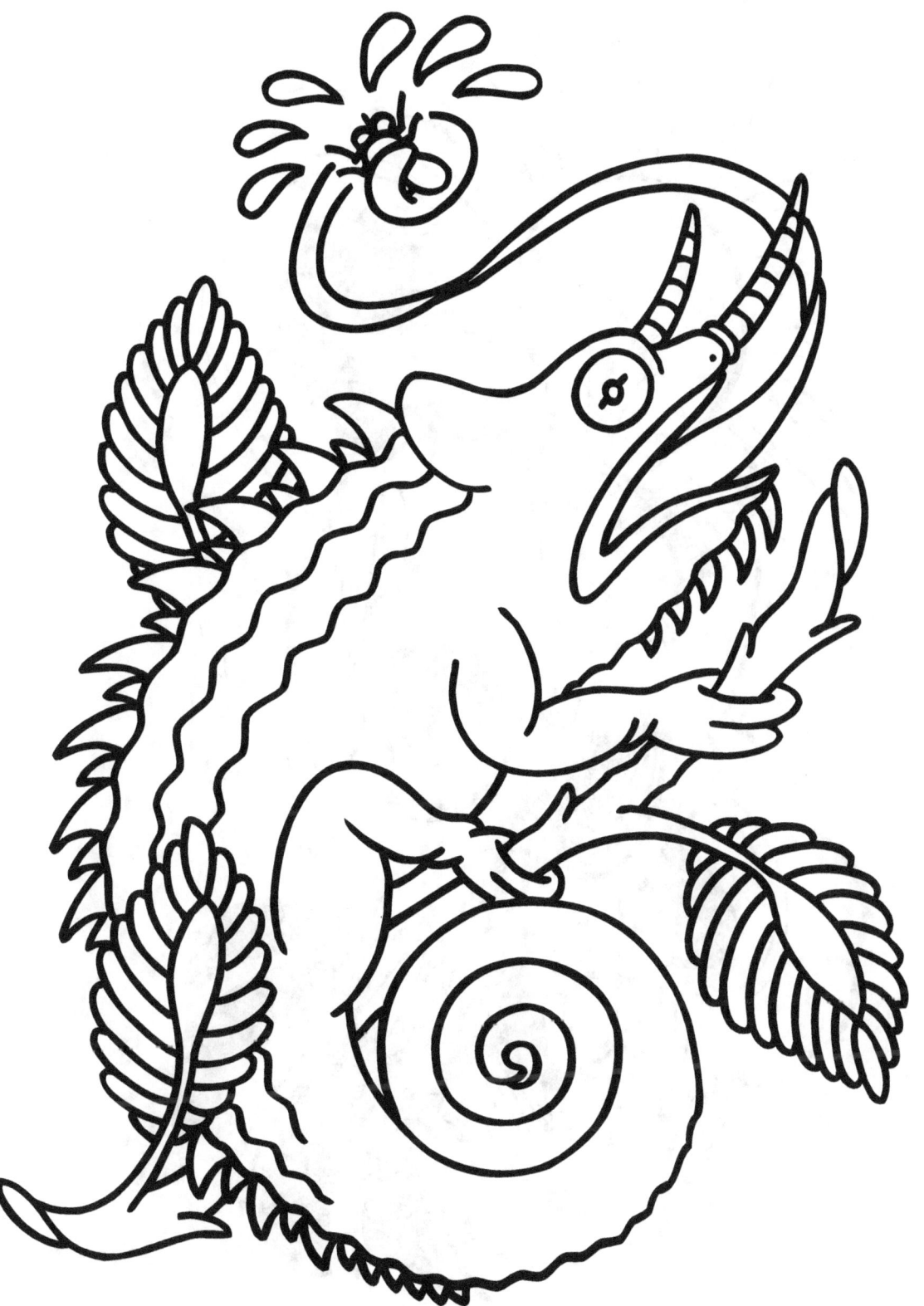

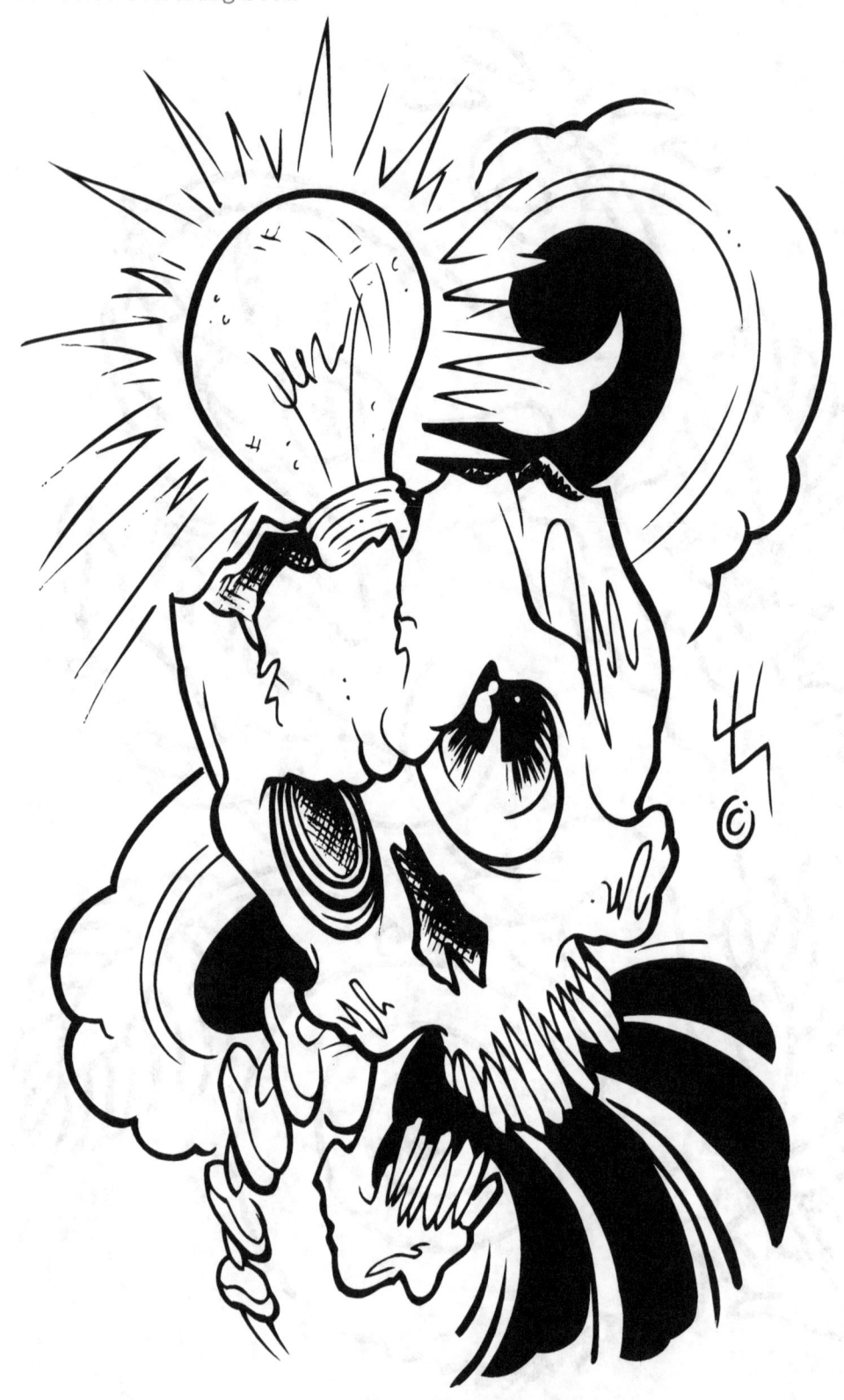

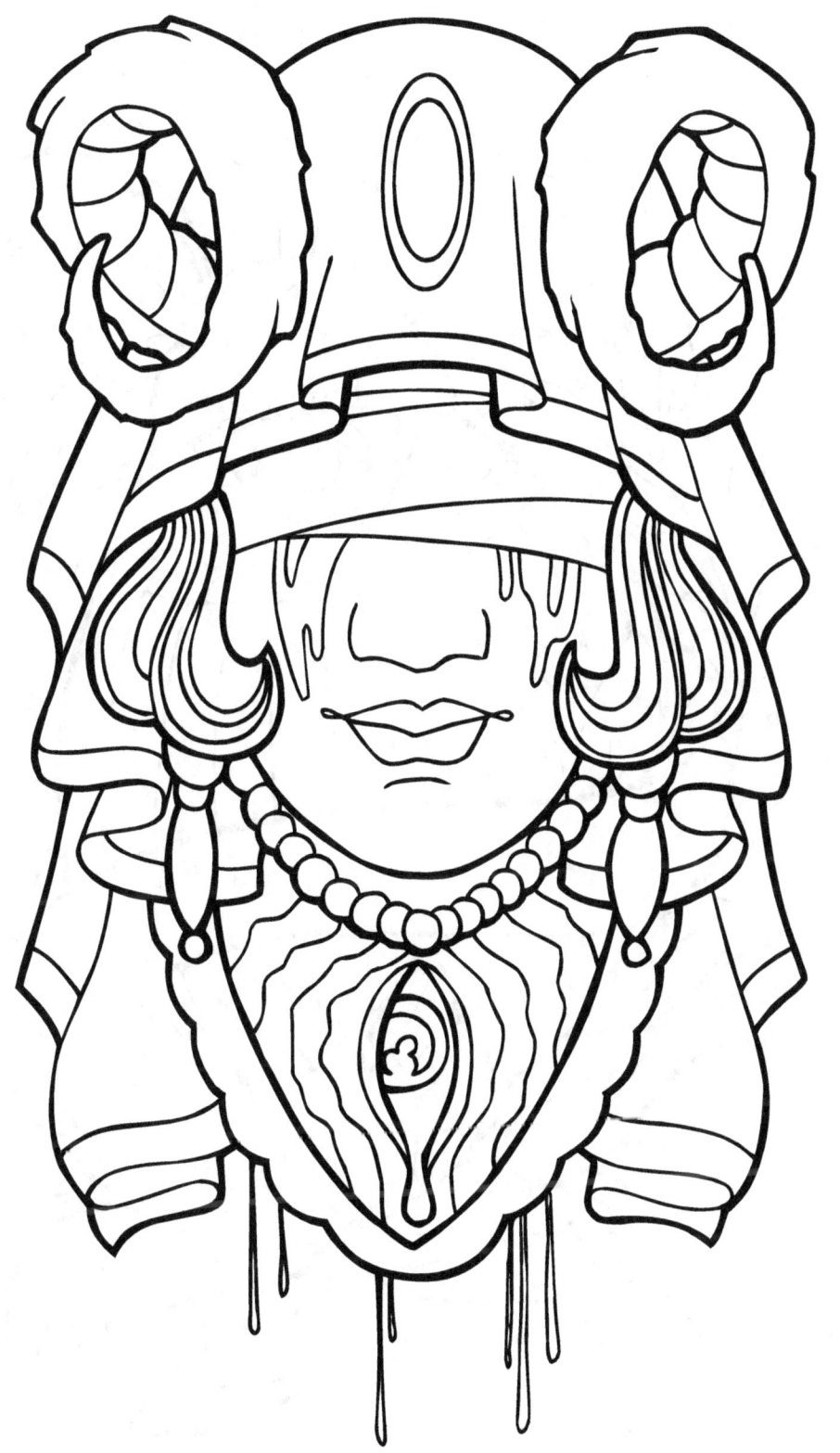

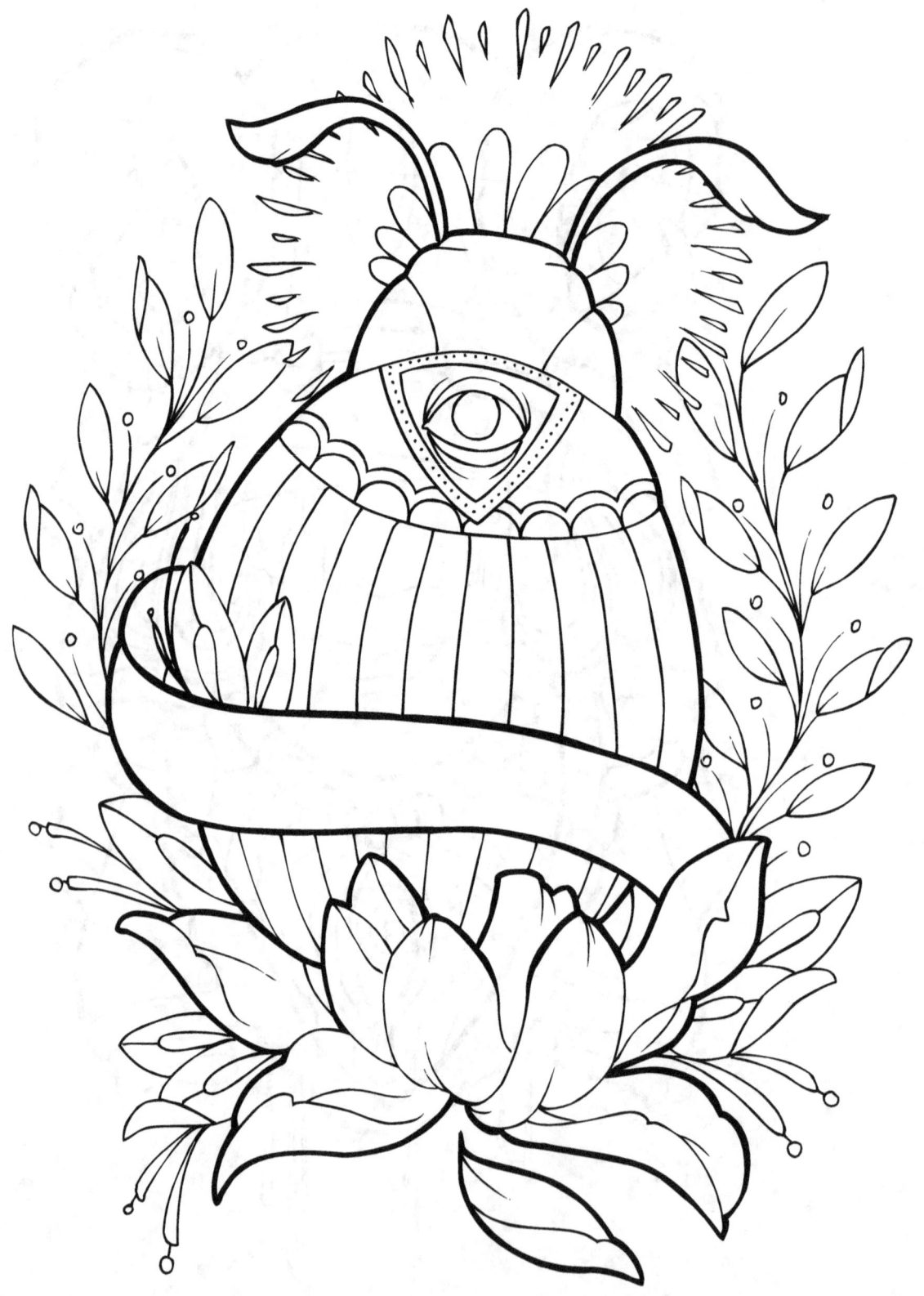

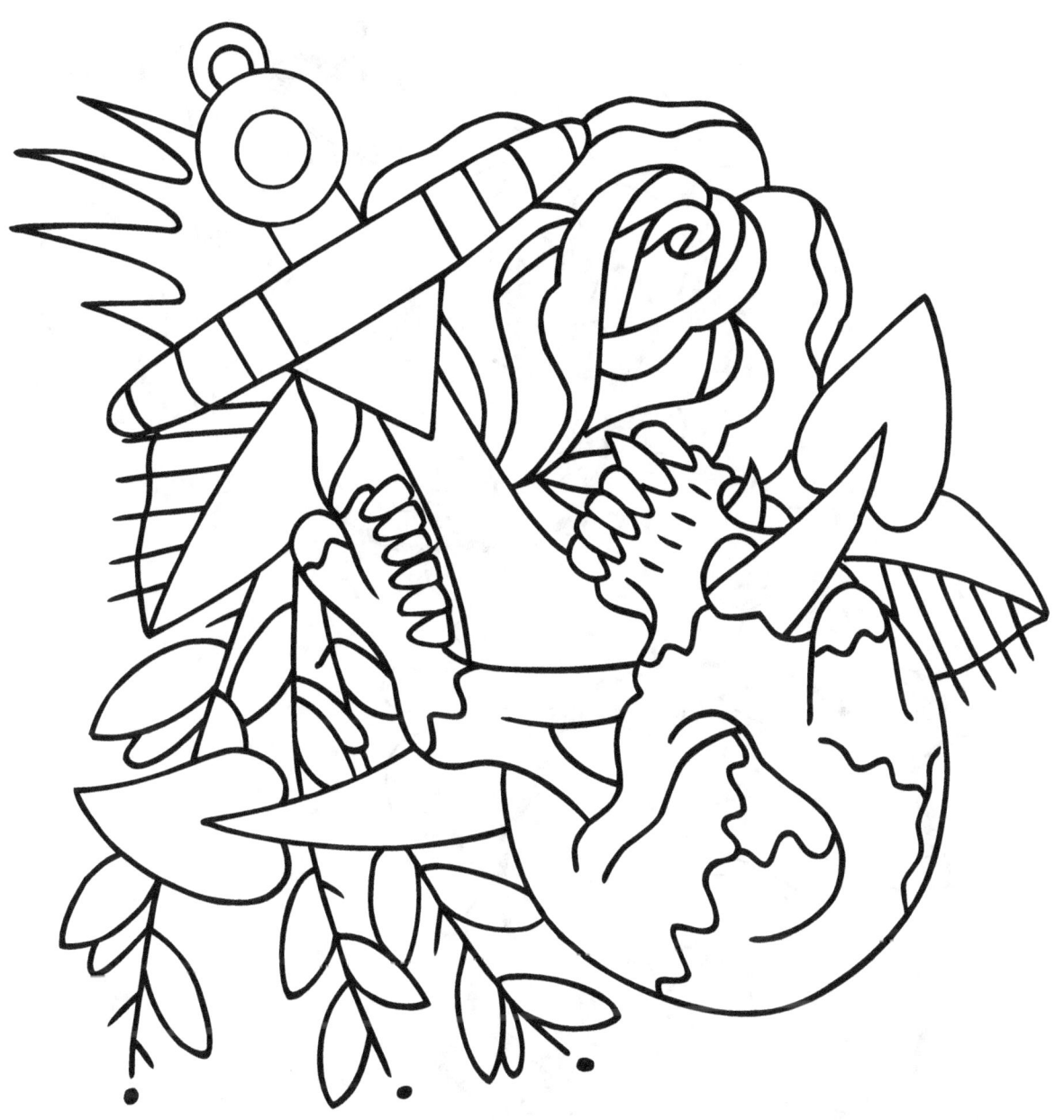

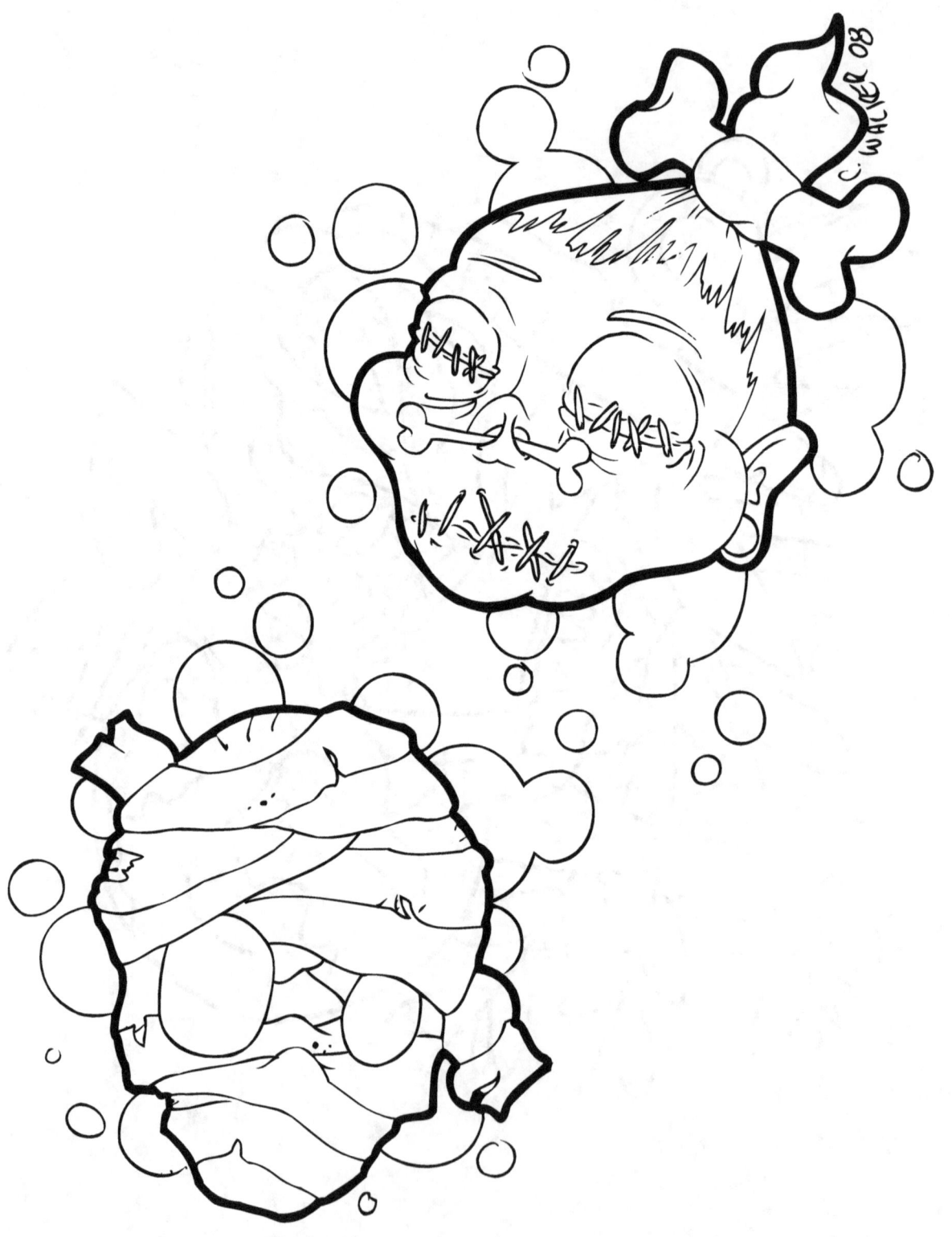

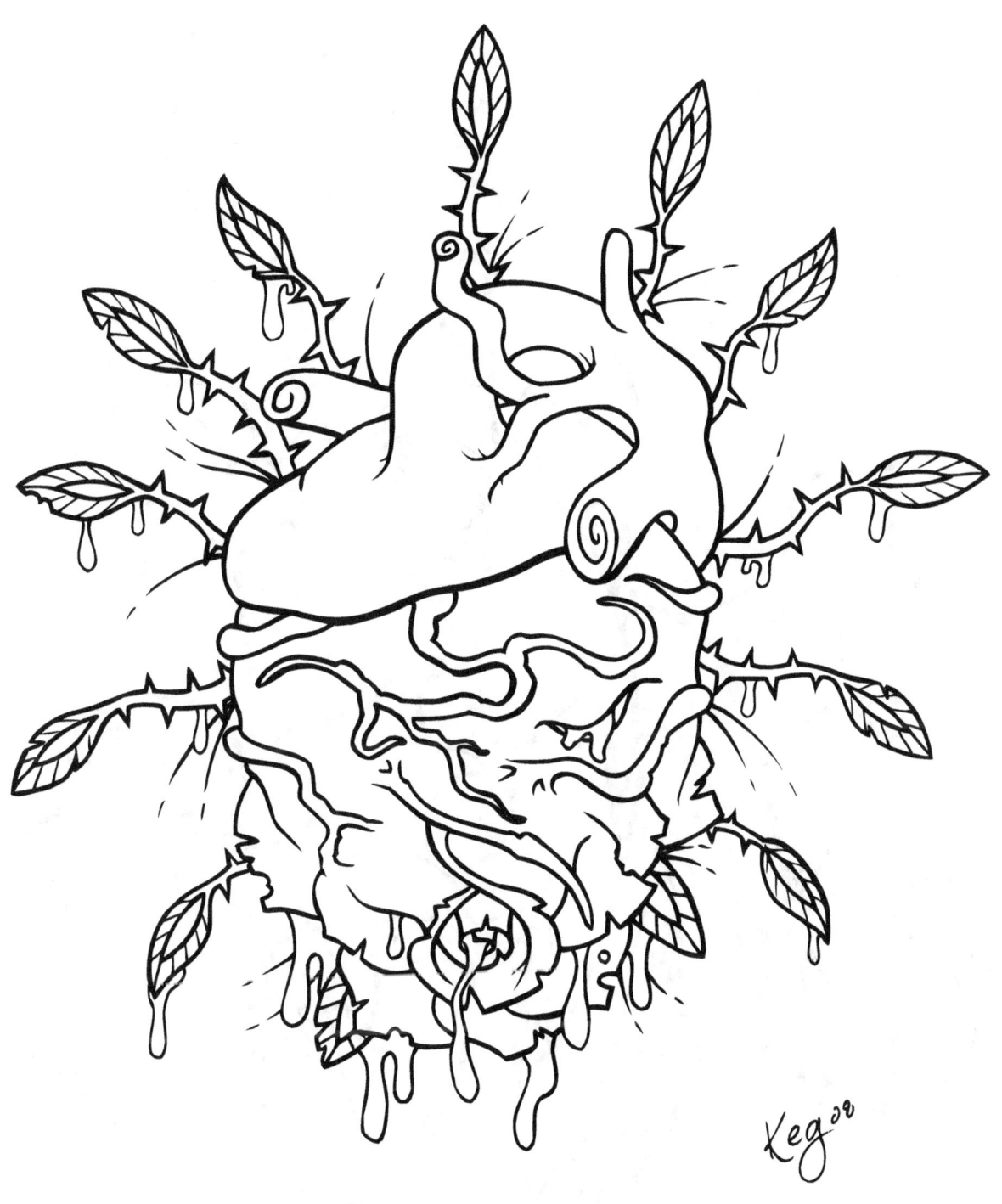

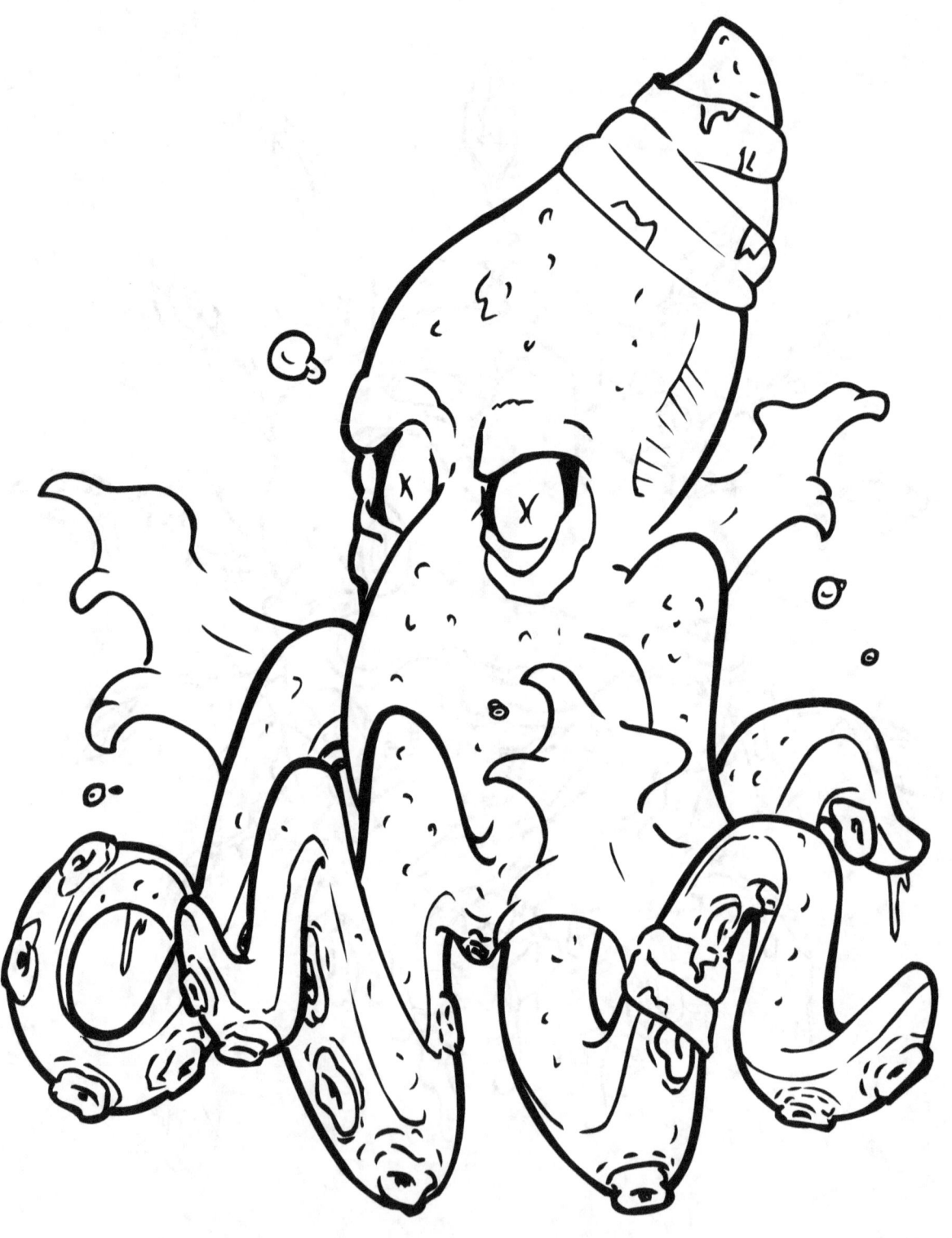

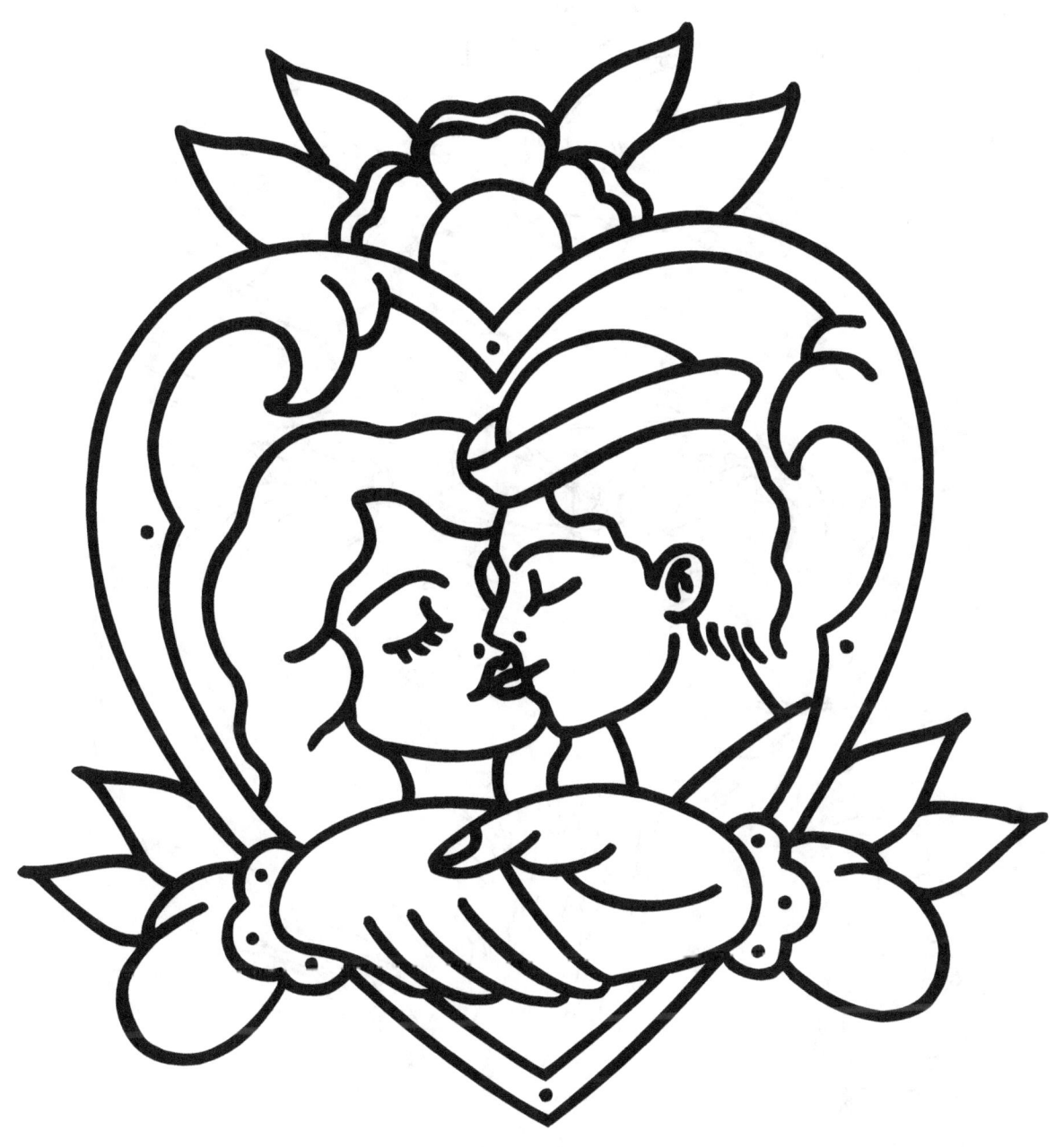

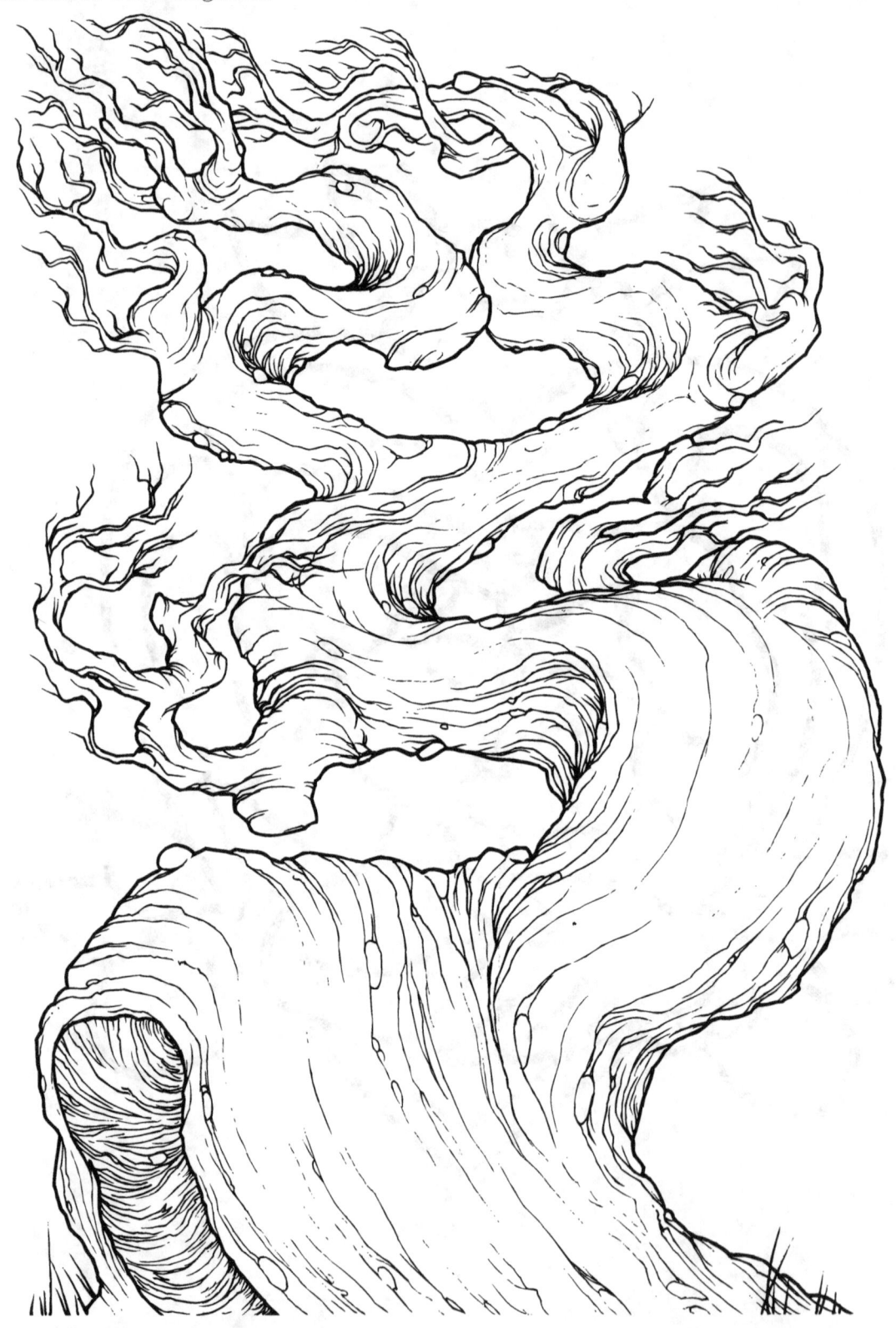

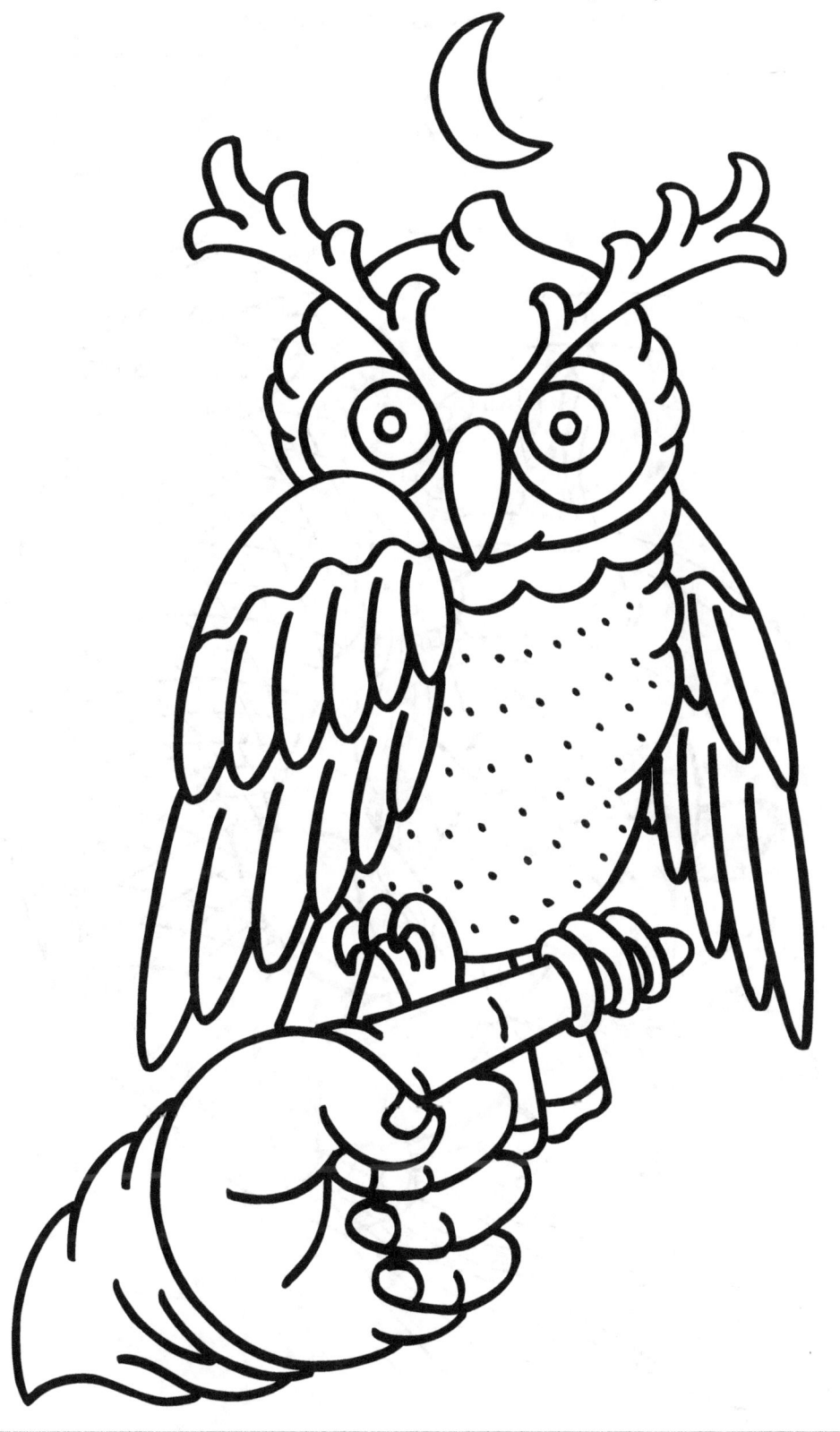

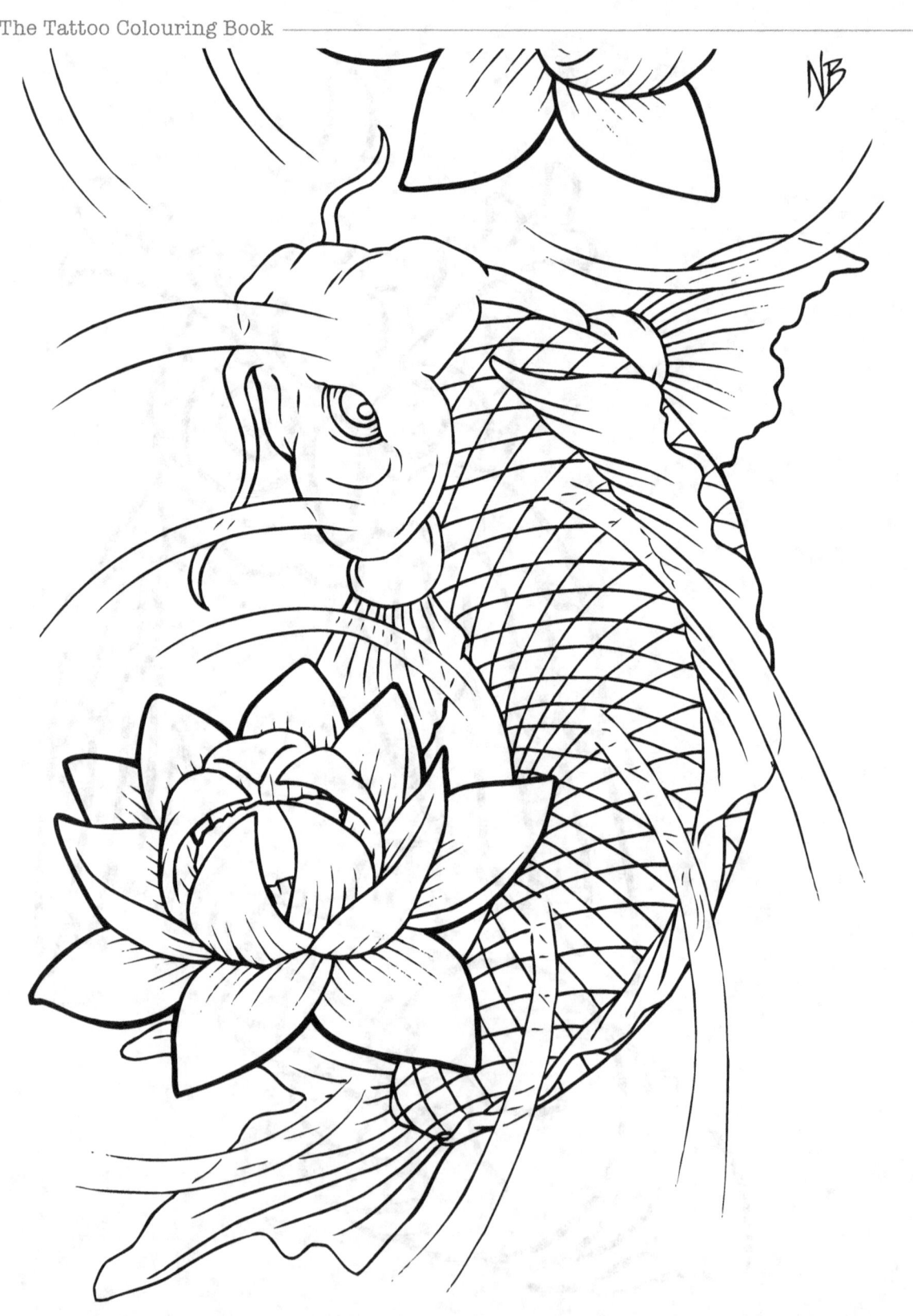

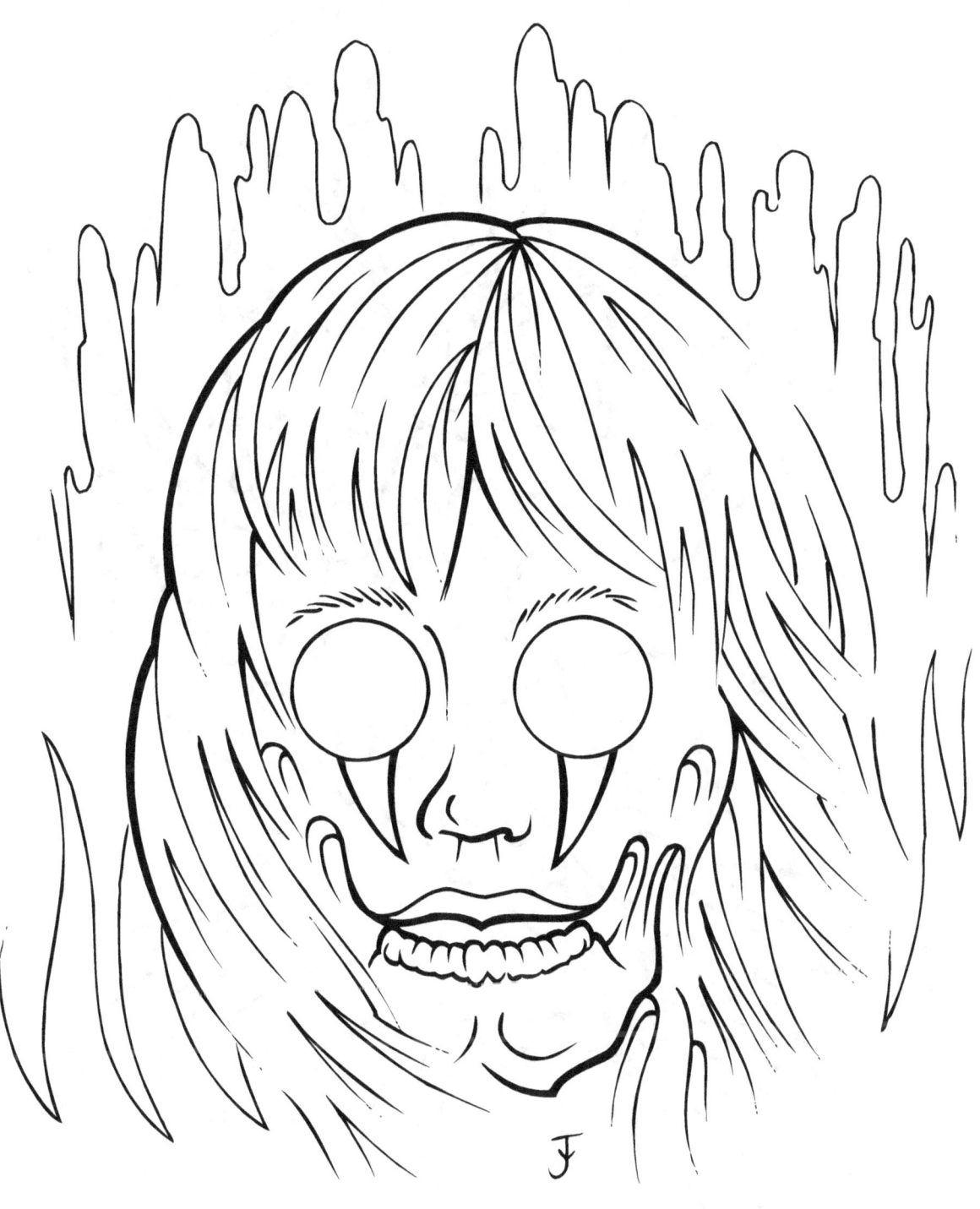

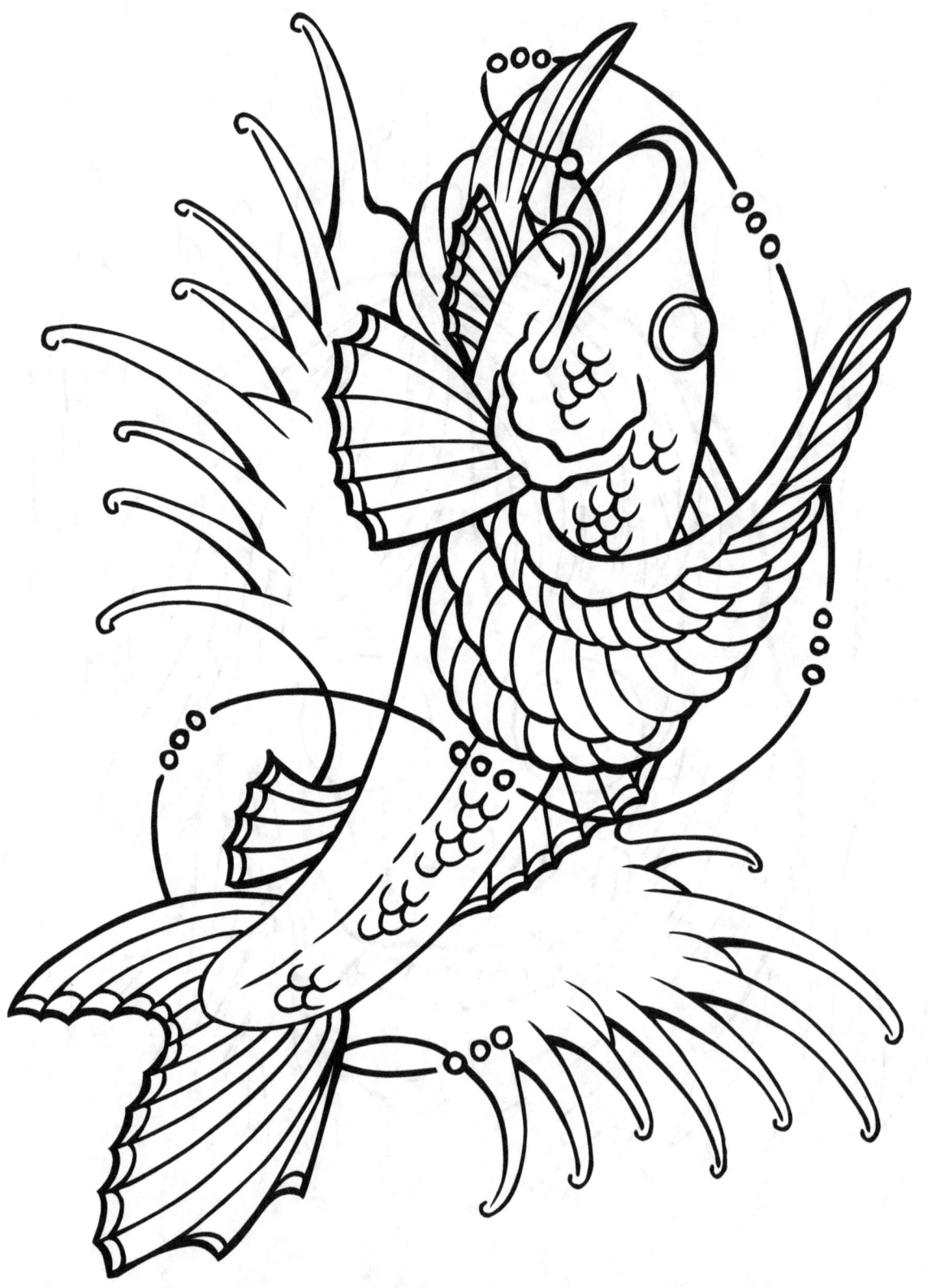

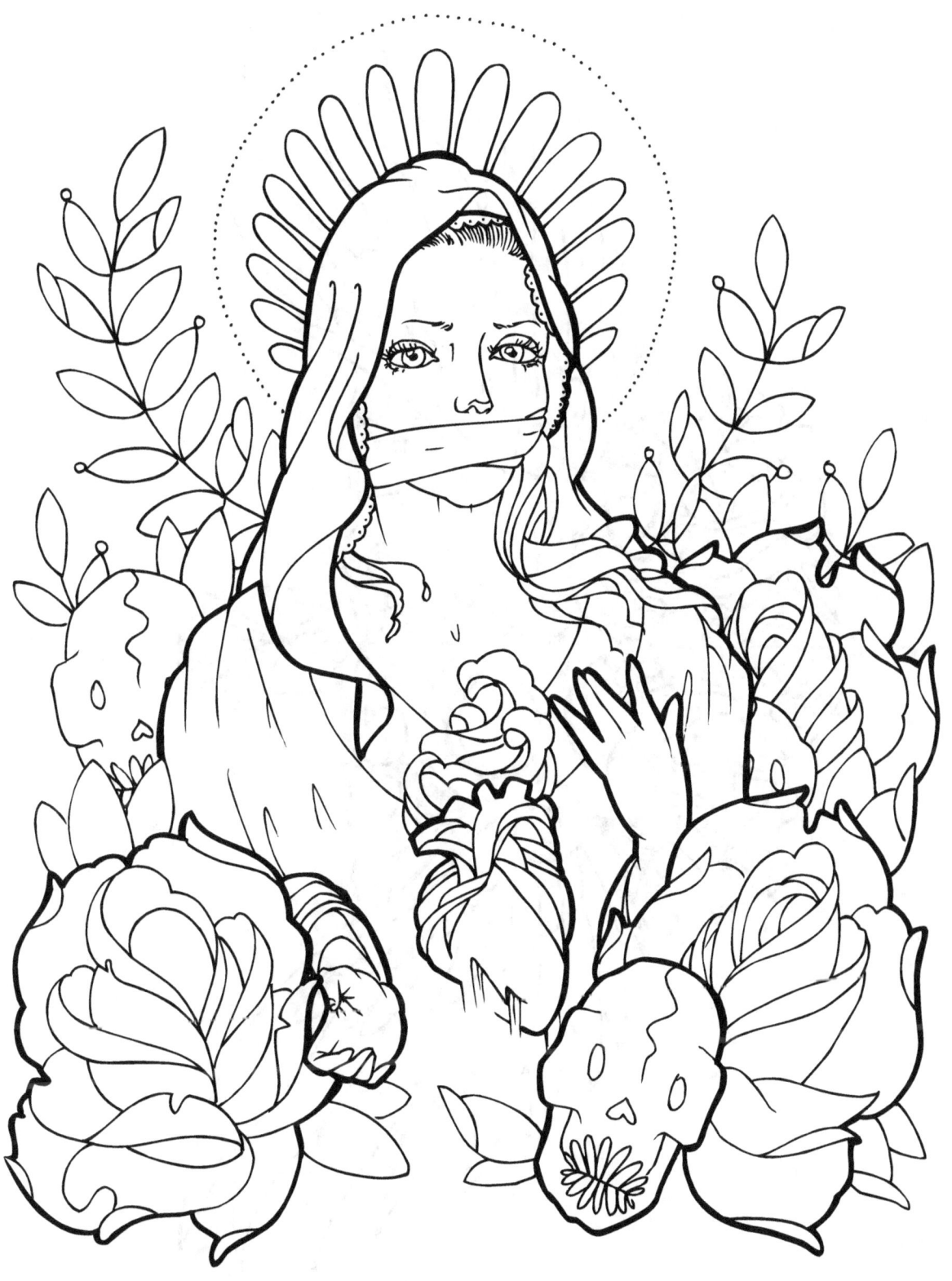

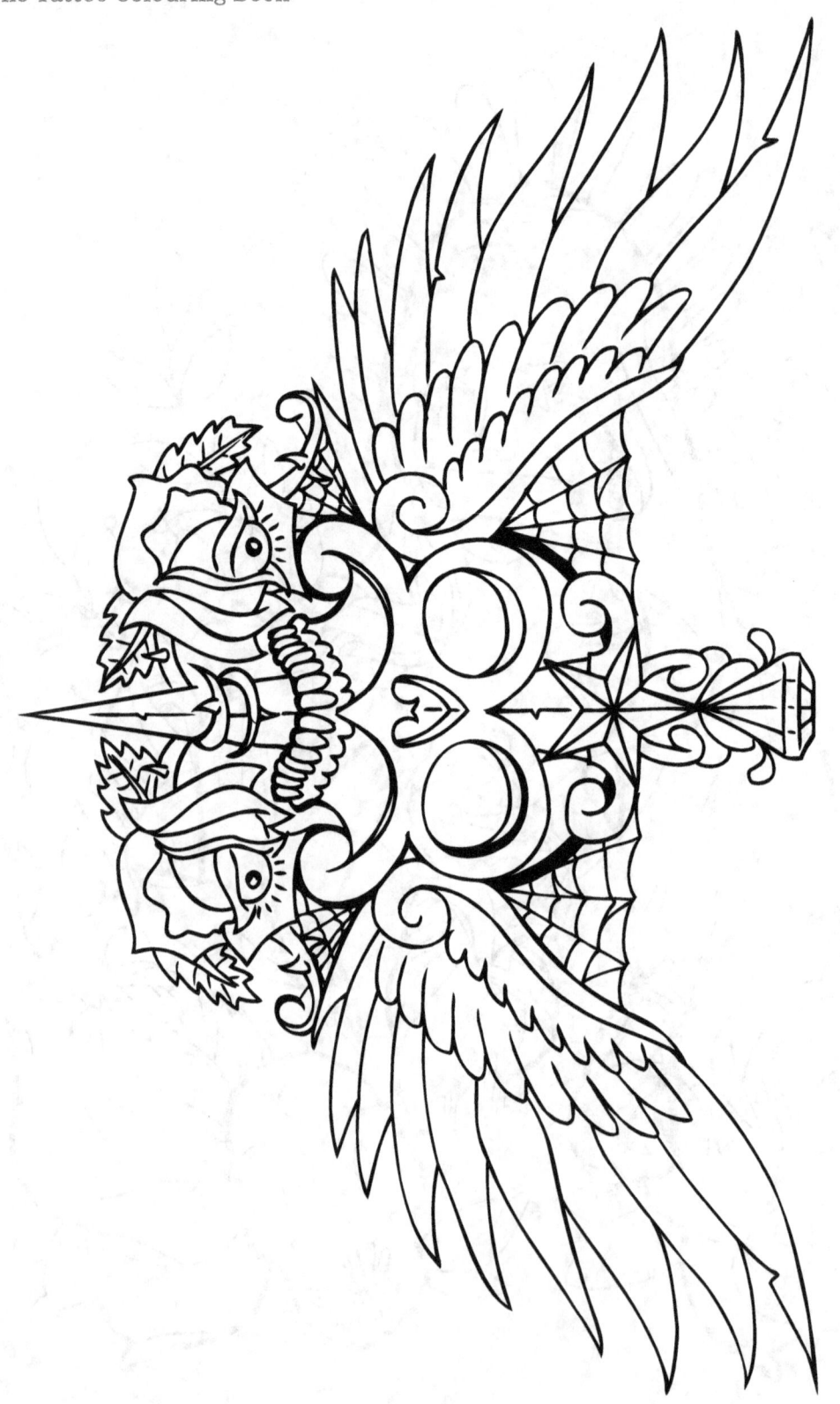

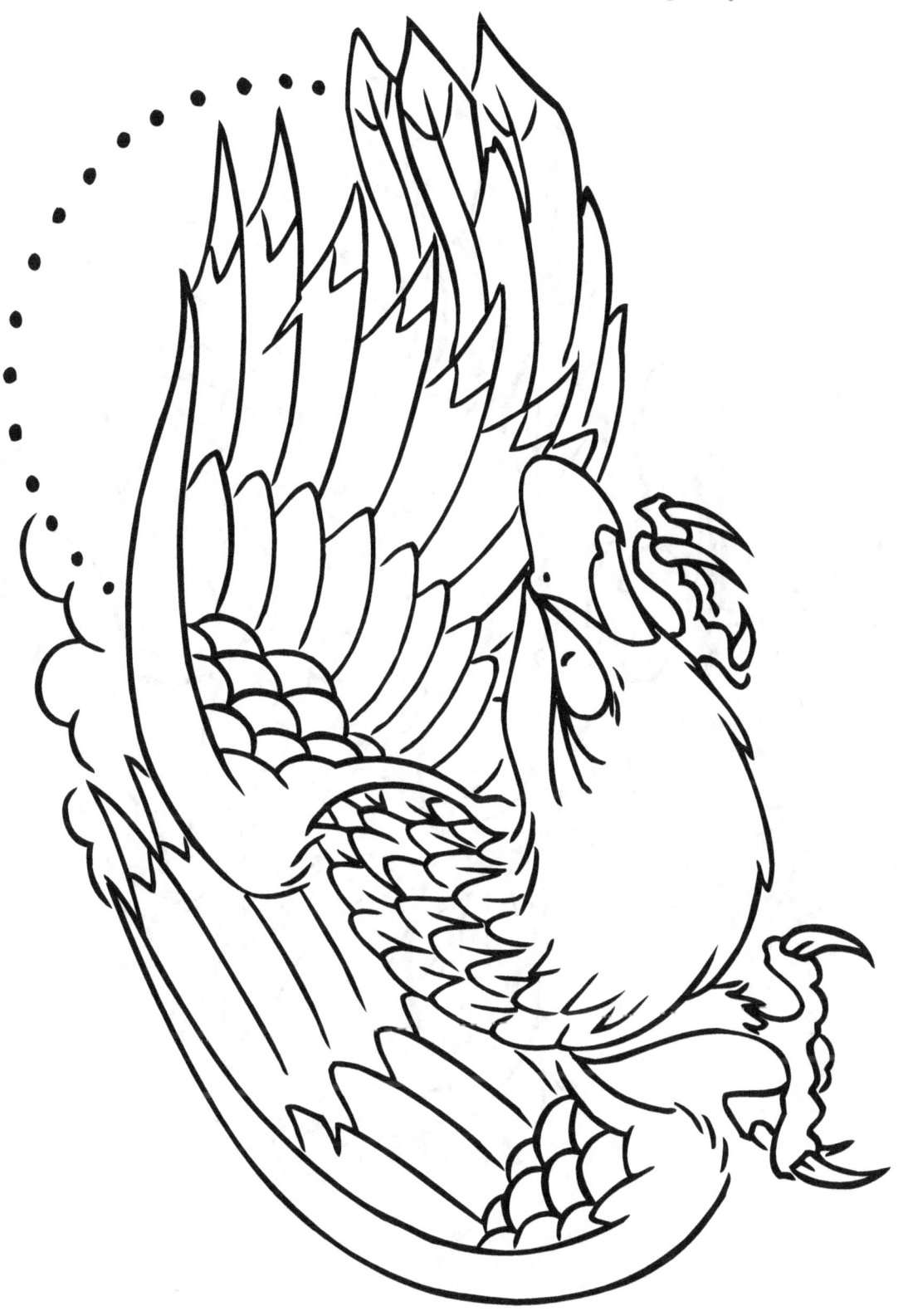

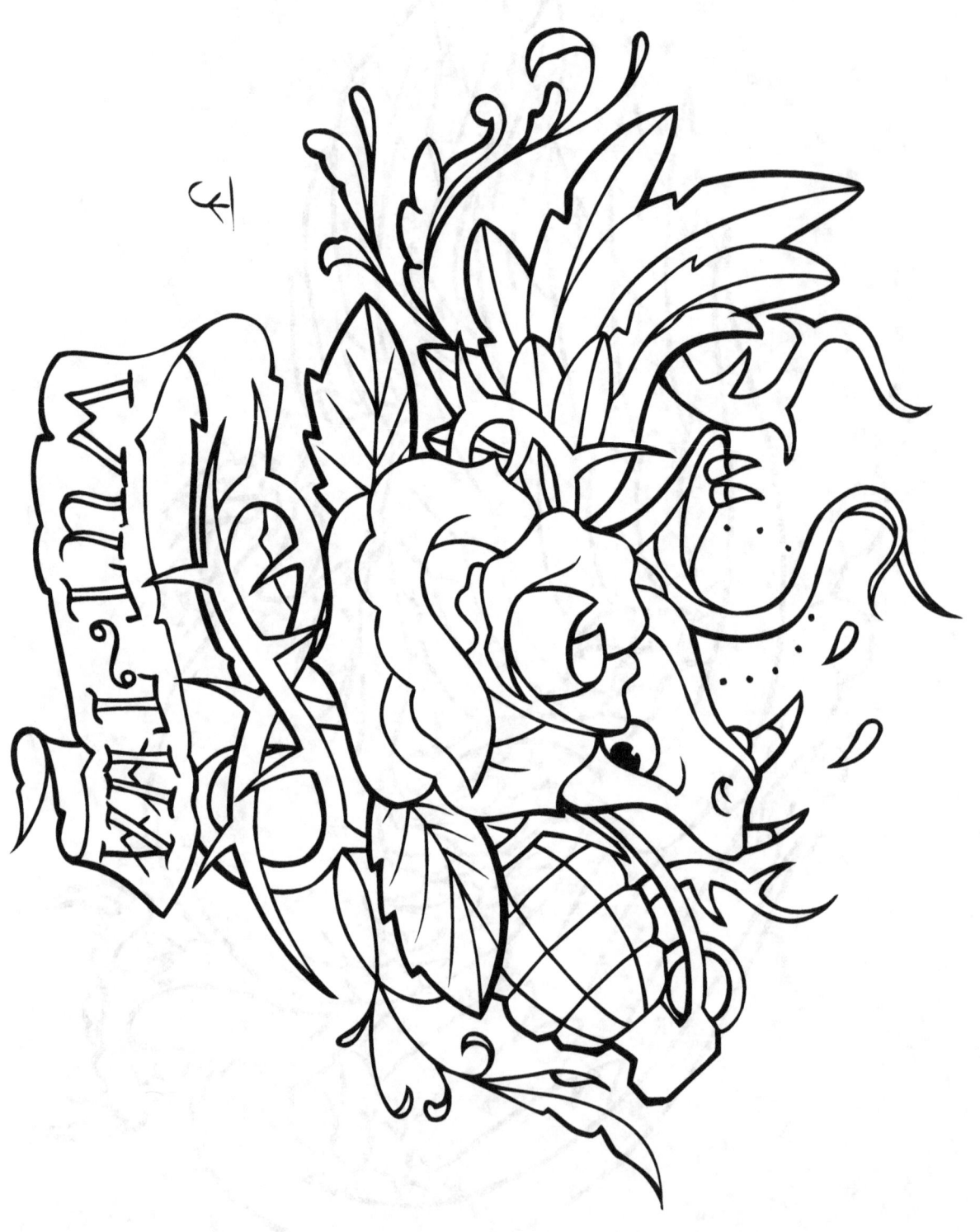

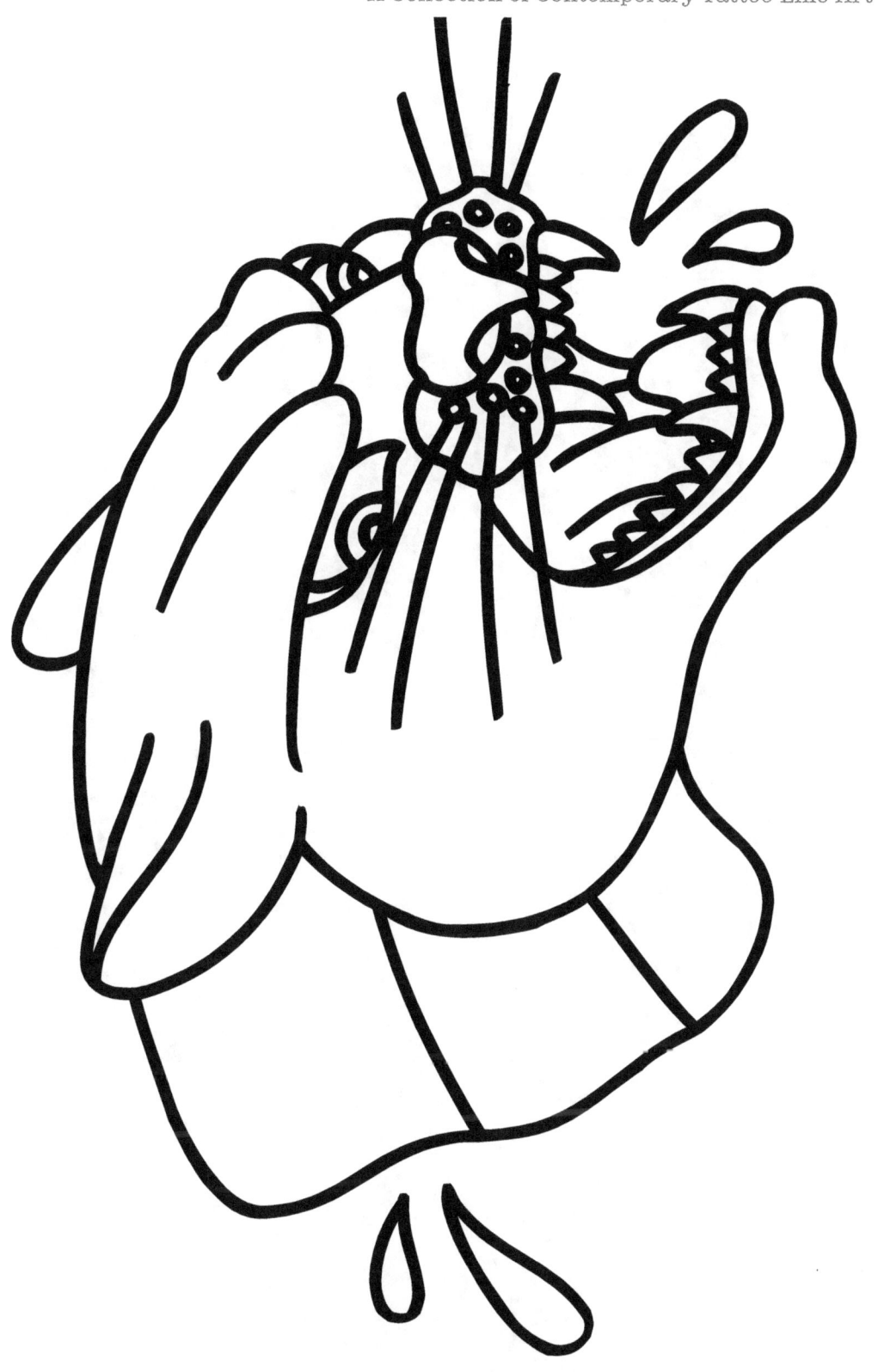

ALSO FROM KIRK & CARA SHEPPARD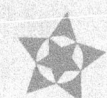

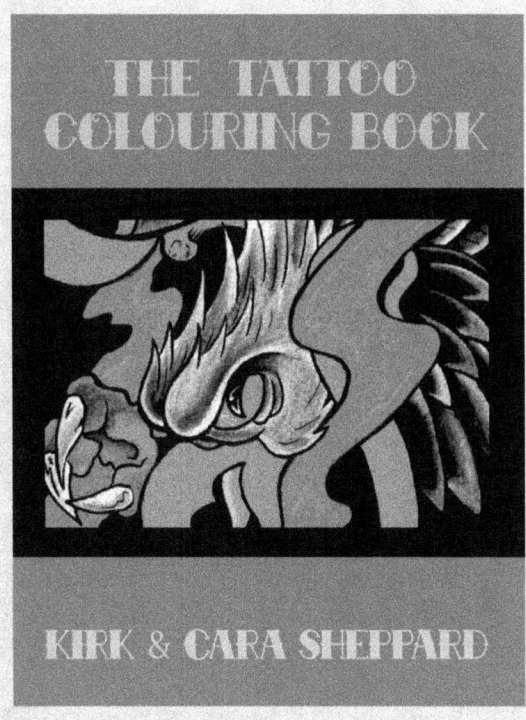

THE TATTOO COLOURING BOOK

May 2005, Trafford Publishing

Fifty-two unique lined tattoo designs, boldly outlined, one per page, and ready for colouring or stencilling. While inspired by traditional North American and Japanese tattoos, each drawing is interpreted with a modern sensibility.

A product of the global tattoo industry today, **The Tattoo Colouring Book** is a quality sourcebook for tattoo artists, collectors, kids, artists, and anyone interested in tattoo art and culture.

Buy **The Tattoo Colouring Book** at www.kidsplayingwithskulls.com

JOIN THE TATTOO COLOURING BOOK COMMUNITY AT WWW.MYSPACE.COM/TATTOOCOLOURINGBOOK

- Post your coloured pages.
- Check out other peoples' work.
- Get the latest reviews of **The Tattoo Colouring Book** and **The Tattoo Colouring Book II**.
- Tell us what you think.

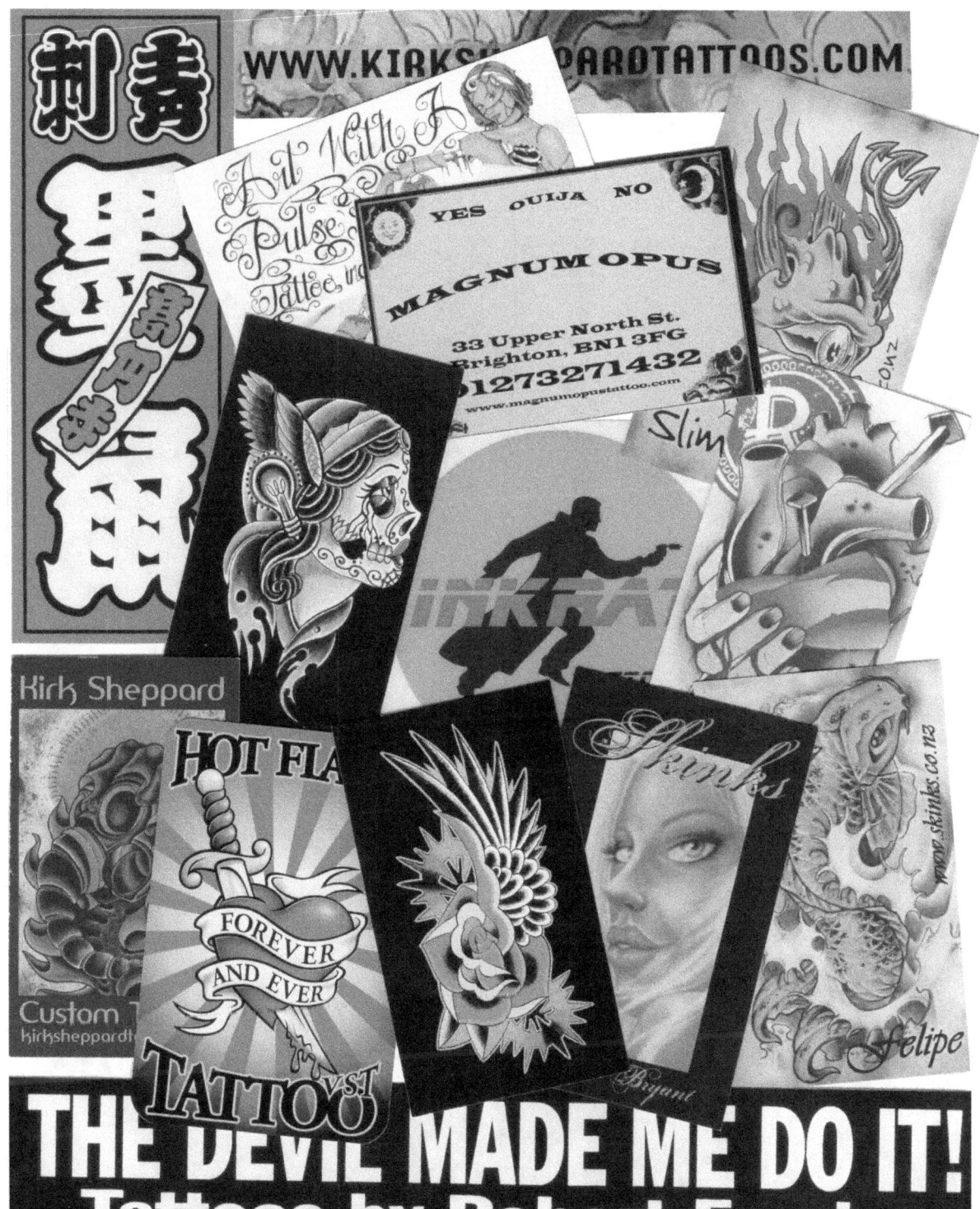